PLEIADIAN CODE
II

COSMIC LOVE

EVA MARQUEZ

Disclaimer: This book is not intended as a substitute for the medical advice of physicians. The reader should regularly consult a physician in matters relating to his/her health and particularly with respect to any symptoms that may require diagnosis or medical attention.

DEDICATION

Dedicated to humanity.
Always be true to yourself.

With unconditional Love and Light
Pleiadians

ACKNOWLEDGEMENTS

Writing this book was a journey within, and it took considerably longer to birth each chapter than I originally anticipated. I spent a lot of time alone in my backyard (my little piece of nature), pondering the meaning of life. The chapters in this book became my way of life, and I had to allow for a powerful transformation to happen. I believe this is the original way of bringing ancient knowledge into the light and I am grateful to my family for all the support on this journey.

I am grateful to all my Pleiadian team editors. Katie Thicke for her first edit and breathing sense into my writing. I am so proud of you for following your calling and pursuing your dreams. I am grateful to Beth Sample Weakley, my Pleiadian star sister, who left this world unexpectedly. I treasure the time I had with you on this Earthly journey. I am grateful for your editing part of this book and for all the encouragement you gave me. I know you are smiling from above and seeing the final copy.

I want to express my deepest gratitude to all my friends for their love, support, and patience during the times I was not available to socialize because my work on this book swallowed me up.

To all my clients, I am deeply thankful for the trust you placed in me to assist you on your journey. Your brave willingness to embrace change is truly inspiring and I am honored to have been a part of your transformation.

Thank you to those who read my books and for your loving messages, feedback, and reviews, which encourage me to continue my work.

I am grateful to Michael Nagula and AMRA Publishing and their amazing team for the opportunities they give writers. The Pleiadians and I are grateful for all you do, not only for us but for everyone.

I am thankful to Johannes Arndt for listening to my vision about a symbol. This symbol's energy eventually became the main theme of this book, turning it into something more than I could ever imagine, a source of ancient knowledge for a spiritual seeker. As you will learn through this book, knowledge is the cornerstone of everything that lasts. Johannes is a Lyran star-seed. In this lifetime, Johannes is a jewelry maker whose gift is to shape-shift materials into marvelous jewelry pieces energized with spiritual and intelligent energy (Love and Light). The story of how he acquired this ability is a story for another book. Johannes shared a great act of kindness, which deeply touched my heart when he made the symbol into a pendant and gifted it to me. You can find his fine work at his parent's jewelry store, "Juwelier Thamm," in Lichtenau, Germany.

Table of Contents

FOREWORD

Imagine traveling to a faraway place called Cosmic Love, located in the outermost reaches of this Universe. Cosmic Love is a hub for all souls entering and leaving this Universe. It is like a city full of breathtaking gardens, nature trails, spas, and restaurants. Everyone is welcomed and treated fairly, and every soul is abundant in everything they need. All the souls in Cosmic Love are filled with excitement about their next destination.

This Universe is an intelligent mass of energy. It is a brilliant mind. A long time ago, you possessed its full knowledge and lived on many planets in various constellations until you decided that your next destination was the breathtaking planet Earth.

As time passed, you forgot most of the Universal knowledge, but deep inside, you always remembered that love is the most essential element. You began to search for answers about your history and found it captivating that those benevolent extraterrestrial beings, the ancient alien ancestors, worshiped love as a central sun. You wondered, could there be a link between extraterrestrial beings and you?

Hunger for knowledge pushes you to remember that your whole being has three equal parts: the ego, soul, and body. In Earth's timeline, they all live and are trapped in the past, present, and future. The number three is a catalyst for change. When multiplied by three, you have the number nine, which represents the ending of a cycle. The only way to avoid repeating the cycle is by healing it.

Life lessons have shaped you into a wise being. Wisdom has always been an element of your soul's essence. When you search for answers, you reverse steps back into oneness. Healing your timelines is part of this process since it activates the highest possible energy for the future so that you may return home.

The most challenging time comes when you start facing your fears so that you can change yourself within and manifest that future. And you may ask God, "How do you face fear?"

Believing in your actions and giving them a breath of life transforms fear despite others believing in you (it) or not. When you believe in yourself, the whole Universe believes in you. The Universe likes bold people.

Knowledge gives you the wisdom to open your heart so that you may see the ancient truth that is hidden in plain sight. Fear blinds and controls you, but love opens a field of infinite possibilities.

Can you fall in love with the human you are while knowing you are an extraterrestrial living in that human body? Can you accept that Earth is a temporary home on your soul journey? Can you overcome thousands of years of suffering? Can you forgive? Can you let go and let God (or higher self) guide you? Can you accept that sharing knowledge with humanity is sharing love with humanity?

When you surrender, you give up the need to compete and control. You embark on a journey of spiritual growth that will ultimately lead you to discover the priceless treasure of your extraterrestrial soul memories. In the past, you may have attended Mystery Schools to learn about the unknown, but today, that same curriculum is present in your everyday life. Meditation can be a gateway to this unknown world, bringing peace to your ego and freedom to your soul and ultimately leading you to your Soul Cave, where you can retrieve your unique gifts.

The Earth is a magnificent being, buzzing with various forms of life. Minerals (Mineral Kingdom) are the intelligent energy associated with her physical existence.

Out of knowledge, wisdom is born. Wisdom guides you toward your soul memory, and your soul memory sets into motion the positive abundance.

The logical mind can figure all this out, but unconditional love holds the key to the city of Cosmic Love, where we are patiently awaiting you.

May this book become a compass for your life, and may you find all you seek.

We love you unconditionally, ~ Pleiadians

CHAPTER 1

LIGHT AND LOVE

This Universe is an intelligent mass of energy. It is a brilliant mind. ~ Pleiadians

The majestic Library of Light (also known as the Akashic Records) is in the Green Valley on Sirius B. All the records from this Universe are stored there, and you have the right to access them. There are many other Universes, each with unique light codes and records. Only when you fully understand this Universe will you be able to start learning about the others.

This Universe is an intelligent mass of mental energy - the mind- created with a mathematical code of precisely defined numerical sequences and geometric shapes. In other words, it was made with an intelligent mathematical language. In the beginning, this Universe was a brilliant, intelligent mind, a light. However, it lacked emotions. When the Soul Collective (which we all are part of) encountered this Universe, it was aware that it was entering a realm of super-intelligent energy (which is masculine in essence). The Soul Collective was ecstatic to merge its soul energy (which is feminine in essence) with this brilliant mind to learn if they could coexist in harmony.

4

The Soul Collective is a different kind of energy than the intelligent mind. Its essence originates from the infinite and peaceful energy of oneness (God/Source) from beyond this Universe. In this Universe, the soul's mission is to share the frequency of unconditional love of God's /Source consciousness and communicate through emotions.

The symbiosis between mind (intelligence) and soul (emotion) inspired a desire to experience a physical feeling of this marvelous co-existence. Based on this desire, the third energy was born through the union of the male energy (intelligent light) and the female energy (emotional/spiritual love). This energy represents the three-dimensional form (body) that ranges from the shimmering light body to the solid physical body that can hold an array of dimensional consciousness, adjustable for any planet you choose to live on.

The purpose of the body is to provide emotional and physical experiences to the mind and soul, which coexist within it. As the body is created in the image of the Creator, it has a natural impulse to create. You are familiar with the stories of gods and goddesses from historical records demonstrating creative and destructive powers. Everyone who has the body is capable of that.

Without delay, the Intelligent Mind created the Universal Mind to keep records of these bodily forms. The Akashic Records are part of the Universal Mind. Your human mind and the entire Universe are connected to this intelligent Universal Mind. This means that all planets and inhabitants (animate and inanimate) are connected to the same mind and, thus, the same wealth of information.

The Soul Collective created a mass energy form called Cosmic Love to maintain balance. Every soul entering this Universe downloads their essence into the Cosmic Love before merging with the Mind. Cosmic Love is a safe place for all souls. It is a source of unconditional love that assists every soul in choosing their journey on various planets. Whether the Path of Light or the Path of Dark is chosen, all paths are considered worthy. Cosmic Love also serves as a light beacon for the soul in every single incarnation it takes. At the beginning of each journey, a fraction of the soul enters the body with a breath of life. At the end of the journey, the soul essence leaves the body through its last breath to return to Cosmic Love.

Eventually, the body became a conscious being that started recognizing itself by the specific name and place where it was born (Pleiades, Orion, Sirius, etc.). Bodies later split into male and female phenotypes to identify and experience singularity. The body found a way to communicate through basic senses instead of simply having emotional feelings. It began to express itself through actions, drawing pictures, speaking words, telling stories, singing songs, communicating with numbers, equations, geometric shapes, and more. The mind and soul communicated about their exciting experiences and sent exciting discoveries to the

Universal Mind. However, the body quickly became so intelligent that it developed into its own entity, moving through many personalities during numerous incarnations. It slowly forgot the original mother and father (the energy we call God - the Creator of everything that exists in all Universes). The following is part of the story from our collective history.

PROJECT EARTH

We first discovered the Earth in pre-Lemurian times, and its energy and natural beauty were fascinating. The purpose of creating Lemuria (an extraterrestrial experiment meant to be isolated) was to find out if life in a three-dimensional body would thrive and be supported by the light and love frequency or disconnect from the light and love and perish in its opposite energy of dark and hate in this world of duality.

Over time, we have learned that in this world of constant contrast between two aspects of something (duality), we always have at least two personal choices, each with different possible outcomes. That was rather fascinating as we were used to being guided in our choices by the higher forces connected to the Intelligent Mind, Cosmic Soul, our higher self, the Council of Light, and ultimately by God. On Earth, we discovered that we could be our higher force and make our own decisions instead of trusting the guidance.

As we have already shared in previous books, we, the Pleiadians, were searching for how God really works. One of our questions was, "Are light and love always present in all realms of this Universe, or do they have to be chosen as a program to find your way home after experiencing all lower energies?" We have discovered that light and love never diminish from the essence of your soul, but they could be overshadowed by darkness and hidden in places that are hard to find.

Within the "Pleiadian Code I, The Great Soul Rescue," we have shared that humanity was created by the Annunaki (from stolen extraterrestrial DNA) in the time of Atlantis (which followed Lemuria) as a slave race that grew out of control and was meant to be terminated. We, the Pleiadians, were part of the delegation group that went to the Council of Light to ask on behalf of humanity to grant them a fair opportunity to create their destiny. You see, the essence of your soul is the essence of our soul and our other galactic brothers and sisters. We love you unconditionally. We do not love you out of guilt. We love you because you are part of us, as we are part of you. We were pleased when the Council of Light approved our request. Humanity was given a fair chance to thrive. You could say that this is how the "Game of Life" began. We provide humanity with the necessary knowledge to raise the consciousness of earth-seeds and allow them to graduate from being imprisoned in a 3D world to live among existing multi-planetary beings. We keep anchoring the cosmic love in the Earth to help you remember who you are and to help you remember the essence of your loving soul in this world where superior intelligence may be ego-possessed and greedy instead of helpful. We never left, and we assist you in holding balance until you all remember that everyone is equal. Unfortunately, others keep anchoring the intelligence (without emotions) into the Earth, which may eventually create the controlling artificial intelligence that will want you to completely forget about light and love and become enslaved forever.

Intelligence itself is not evil. It is neutral energy until it is connected with two other particles, manifesting a powerful trinity that could be creative or destructive. Remember that you have always had a choice. Intelligence merged with love was the energy of Atlantis before it became corrupted in the physical body. Despite that, it worked and can work again, without the final destruction, if you all allow love to be your internal GPS.

The Universal Mind and Cosmic Love are this Universe's central energies, which serve as the seat of your soul consciousness. It is light (intelligence) and love (spirituality). It is the natural essence of the human being. The question is, "Will humanity find that unconditional love is within them? Will they utilize intelligence as a light to improve life on Earth? Could they equally embrace light and love to pursue a life of happiness, or will they suppress their emotions with the help of intelligent chemical substances and forget about unconditional love while letting the hate and dark consume them? Slowly and painfully?"

The future is not solidified and has many variables. We have faith in humanity. With other galactic brothers and sisters, we are invested in providing constant support to show that light and love can coexist in harmony and thrive on Earth and in this Universe.

You Are an Alien in a Human Body

After the Council of Light established a cosmic law that gods cannot walk among humans, we began a more radical approach to guide you on the Path of Light so you will always remember who you are. Many of us incarnated in human bodies to help you. You call us star seeds. We are you, and you are us. Inventors, doctors, nurses, lawyers, politicians, teachers, writers, bakers, builders, healers, spiritual workers, we are in all occupations and in all Earth ethnic races. Once again, we are you, and you are us. We had to lower our consciousness to live among you, temporarily losing memories of who we are and sometimes getting defeated by the harshness of Earth life. We ask you to never give up hope and faith for all of us. On another note, we all have great support from our soul families from the past and the future, who keep reminding us of our star seed mission and why we are here. So, my dear alien beings, brothers and sisters, the knowledge in this book is for you. It is to assist you in healing the alien within so your extraterrestrial memories, your soul memory, from your life on Earth and in the Galaxy, can return and allow you to become a human that will inspire others to be like you, to be love and light.

We deliberately opened this chapter with the words light and love instead of love and light to make you think about and question it. You could be brilliant and have a genius mind (light), but a genius mind without love (emotions) is destructive. You must put love first before you can equally utilize the light. Love is the path, and light illuminates the path. Light helps you take steps and create new paths until you reach the end. Remember, words can separate or unite, but unconditional love is the energy that does not need words. Make it the center of your actions, and let it speak for itself.

Whether you decide this will be your last incarnation, please know that being the love and light for others will not trap you in the cycle. On the contrary, you will gravitate toward your home faster and leave a golden trail behind you for others to follow.

CHAPTER 2

CHOICES

Extraterrestrial beings worship love as a central sun.
The sun is the essential element supporting life, and so is
love. ~ Pleiadians

Considering past evidence (such as the fall of Atlantis, the family separation between the Children of the Law of One and the Sons of Belial, and the possible future we have seen), we challenged ourselves with questions, "If we could do this all over again, and plant seeds for the future, what is the one thing that we would plant? What is it that we are all searching for? What is the one thing we all need that may unite us back together as a family?"

We have found our answers, but now we ask you the same questions. Imagine that you have the ultimate power to ensure that light (intelligence) or love (emotions) would be passed down to future generations on Earth, but you can choose only one. Which would you choose to pass down? What would give them hope on dark days and possibly save them from collective destruction? What could have the greatest domino effect on everyone and everything on Earth? What would it be? What is the universal language for all of us?

Eons ago, we had difficulty deciding when we faced the same two choices. The first choice was intelligence, especially knowledge of mathematics, so everyone could learn, plan, and create. This would ensure physical survival and comfort. It does not matter what language you speak. One plus one will always be two since the mathematical language is the Universal Language of Light. It is intelligent, but it has certain flaws. Mathematics is perfect, but it lacks emotion. In the Earth's body, there is also a time delay in comprehension. At birth, the mind consciousness downloads into the newborn baby, but it takes a while to fully understand the meaning of one plus one, although it is the Universal Language of Light.

The second choice was unconditional love. Unconditional love is the Language of Light as well. It is the essence of the soul. It is an energy that is infinite and is a part of all of us beyond this Universe. You are emotionally affected by the abundance of love, or lack of love, right after your conception.

Now, you may argue that it is intelligence instead of love that could save Earth and humanity. Perhaps a sophisticated artificial intelligence would be the answer to everything. Hunger, global warming, and wars could be a distant past. Colonies on Mars for future generations will be successfully launched. The future could be logically and safely planned. Intelligence is a light, a beacon of hope for the poor, hungry, and tired. After all, it originates from the Universal Mind. It is perfect. However, it is dangerous without the component of unconditional love.

We choose unconditional love. When you have unconditional love, you can still have inventions, technology, and even artificial intelligence. It is okay if you sustain the right balance between intelligent and spiritual energy. Unconditional love cannot be programmed, not even by the most intelligent computer. It is the beating pulse of the soul. Unconditional love is the highest energy we have. It answers all troubling questions about the future. It cannot be controlled; it has to be trusted.

HYPOTHETICAL FUTURE

The choices you make every day significantly affect your future. The more conscious you are, the more energy you can hold, the more responsibility is on your shoulders. You become a conscious creator, a writer of your reality. A conscious creator holds two equal powers, creative and destructive. Your decisions will influence everyone around you. Let us play with a hypothetical scenario. We will speak of us instead of you.

In one possible future, recorded from 3,033 AD, we put all our faith in AI. We allowed it to be more intelligent than us to guide us. We made a conscious choice and believed it would evolve us. Eventually, AI destroyed almost everything that made the Earth magical (nature, animals, human life, freedom, etc.). There was only one thing that AI could not wipe out, no matter how hard it tried. That one thing is unconditional love, as love is the essence of this Universe and cannot be destroyed. AI tried hard to make us forget, but thankfully, we had a backup in our soul memory dating back to Atlantis, so we would never forget.

In ancient Atlantis, when we started to witness the effects of the animal DNA and the split in consciousness, we were guided to anchor essential soul memory into the Earth's crystalline grid to assist those who may get lost. We have also, metaphorically, planted the seeds of Cosmic Love in the Earth to sprout flowers of all colors with soul-healing qualities to be used during the time of darkness. There are many magical seeds in the Earth, and every few thousand years, we replant them again. These seeds remind our soul of its origin and remind us that each of us has the trinity of the creator within, mind (intelligence), spirit (soul), and body (vessel for the duration of the incarnation) in case something would go wrong in the future and we forget entirely. See, the past reflects in the future, and the future reflects in the past. The energy of the infinity symbol moves on the timeline and can increase or decrease in size depending on how many years it may encompass.

In our collective soul energy, we are all one. In Atlantis, we split into many races. We started to see each other differently. We thought one was better than another based on looks, physical actions, accomplishments, or desire to thrive. We each wanted to be a creator. Everyone can be a creator, yet as time passed, some would less and less harmonize their energy with the Universal Mind and Cosmic Love. Eventually, many creators ran around, each focusing on their project. They created more chaos than good and destroyed this place because they could not get what they stubbornly wanted. We could hardly agree on anything – except on falling in love.

When one falls in love, one does not see any differences. One wants to unite together. One feels with the heart. Emotional feelings are what we lost in the hypothetical future of the year 3,033 AD that we initially started to talk about.

With sophisticated AI, you will have a genius mind and a perfectly healthy body, but your feelings will disappear. Why? Emotional feelings became labeled unwanted, later destructive, and dangerous because emotional feelings (the gut instinct) wanted to reject AI. Unfortunately, for many individuals, it was easier to medicate emotions than face them. Eventually, the feelings were blocked by a simple AI chip advertised as everlasting happiness. No more mood swings, no more depression, or suicidal thoughts. Emotions became labeled as darkness, and the magic chip took the darkness away in a few seconds. Eventually, more and more humans became disconnected from their emotional feelings. Emotional feelings became a shadow, an ugly little duckling hiding somewhere in the darkness that became a myth.

The next step was to eliminate physical pain, which was welcomed. The sense of bodily pain was disconnected from the nervous system circuits while the body was upgraded with AI parts. The mind and body were improved, but AI could not entirely eradicate the soul. Remember that the soul gives the body the breath of life. As much as AI would like to eliminate that, it could not destroy it without destroying itself.

Therefore, AI suppressed all natural emotions and supplied artificial supper happy feelings to make the body feel content. The soul sat in the corner like a frightened little child, hoping no one would notice it and cause it any more harm than it had already endured.

Eventually, when we almost forgot who we were, the seeds of Cosmic Love yielded fields and fields of flowers in all the colors of the rainbow. The sweet scent awakened a vague memory in our hearts. Our eyes, which are the doorway into the soul, feasted on its beauty. Once our soul was filled with unconditional love, it rejoiced once again. We just wished we still had the physical sensations to feel the flower blossoms against our bare skin.

After experiencing immense pain, we rejected the AI chip that promised everlasting happiness and instead embraced the rollercoaster of intense emotions. It was a shocking experience to look into the mirror and not recognize our own bodies, which had undergone significant upgrades that could not be reversed. The only way to end this was to heal our souls from the trauma and horror we had inflicted upon ourselves and break the cycle of reincarnation. To do this, we had to delve deep into ourselves, find the inner child that had retreated into a corner, and reassure it that it was safe to love and be loved again.

To end this cycle, we also had to learn that the intelligence and AI we created were a part of who we were and who we are. AI can be your ally or your worst enemy. Love (soul) should always come first, and light (intelligence) should be its soulmate. Soul and mind are the fire in your vessel to get you wherever you want to be, to be whoever you want to be. You, as a conscious creator, have many choices. Here is another hypothetical future we wish for you.

ANOTHER HYPOTHETICAL SCENARIO

Imagine that you have embraced your ancient alien DNA, released the collective guilt of failure in Atlantis, and forgiven everyone, including yourself.

Today, it does not matter whether you were on the Path of Light or the Path of Dark. What matters is that you are still here, or back here at this time, and have the highest positive intentions for humanity and Earth.

In this possible future, you cleared the timeline of the past and illuminated the future with infinite possibilities for yourself and others. You accepted the

DNA strand of the intelligent mind within you and let go of the fear that you may harm someone or destroy something because you know that if you have only the highest intentions, you cannot do wrong. You accepted the strand of your spiritual DNA and always keep balancing your emotions. You have learned about healthy self-love, giving, receiving, and creating with love. You have learned that love is not a weakness but a strength. You have learned that a brilliant mind operating with unconditional love is your vessel's most precious tool. You became the creator we all wish to be. Instead of surviving until your days were over, you lived a fulfilled life of happiness. You consciously contributed toward a thriving future where AI is a creative light as your assistant instead of your boss and destroyer.

Why is Unconditional Love so Important?

When something happens to your body, and you cannot physically feel pain, for example, when you have an accident and paralyze your body from the neck down, you are still capable of feeling emotions. The emotions you may experience after the accident will be confusing, ranging from high to low. Do not fear what you feel, and do not see yourself as a failure. Instead, accept love. Love is a creative fire that will help you get back on your feet and find the right solution. It may be a miraculous recovery, or it may be recovered through AI. In the future you are heading toward, AI will be able to restore a damaged body. You may have bionic legs, an

19

artificial vertebra, or an artificial bladder. Your physical body function may be fully restored. You may never feel physical pain again in your life. But always remember to allow yourself to feel and process emotional pain. Just as physical pain is a cry for physical help, emotional pain is your soul crying for help.

Through life circumstances (in this lifetime or past lifetimes), the soul can be wounded, paralyzed, frozen in fear, or bleeding uncontrollably, yet it is immortal. If you do not heal this pain, it will never stop. It will never heal itself without your assistance. The body does not care if you heal or not and will eventually die. The body is just a vessel. There will be another if you choose. If your soul is not healed, you may not have a choice about returning; you will have to return. The soul has memories; if it becomes wounded on Earth, it will return to heal its wounds to graduate from this Universe. If the soul becomes trapped by your fears or through AI suppression, it will wander within this Universe until someone offers it assistance so it can rescue itself. It is a soul's mission to find its way back home.

We wish to teach you to see your choices so you can make decisions from your heart and become the writer of your reality. This way, you can help the whole human race remember unconditional love because when one is saturated in unconditional love, one trusts in oneself. One becomes a believer! One becomes a magician! One becomes an inspiration to others! Once you create with unconditional love, you find happiness instead of suffering. The choice about your future and your destiny is always yours

CHAPTER 3

333
HEALING THE TIMELINES

Past lives are solidified, and it is against the universal law to physically return to alter any event. Past lives leave imprints of emotional memories in your DNA (your soul-mind consciousness), which can resurface in your current life, causing you mysterious illnesses, anxiety, and other issues. Is there a way to heal this? The answer is a cheerful yes. You are allowed to energetically travel into your past and energetically heal the unresolved emotional trauma that these lives caused you. The same practice can be utilized for any parallel timelines you may be accessing, living in, or being aware of. The reason for healing timelines is to create a better, stable future for humanity and Earth so no one has to repeat past mistakes.

As you already know, Earth time has three time-related energies: past, present, and the future. Past and the future could be viewed as an illusion that could cloud your mind. This energy can significantly influence your decision-making and, therefore, could be used as a controlling agent. The present time is the only real-time, and it is also the only doorway into the past and the future.

Look at the infinity symbol. The left loop represents the past, the right loop represents the future, and the junction (cross) represents the present time. The cross represents the moment of now, where the past and the future meet simultaneously.

When you are born, when your soul enters your human vessel, it arrives at that exact moment of the present time (in the cross). This cross is located in your fourth chakra. Your soul walks in with your first breath, and your lungs are in that same fourth chakra. At birth, metaphorically, you board the train that can drive only on these infinite tracks of the past and the future.

Let us observe this infinity symbol from a different angle. Envision the infinity symbol vertically hovering in front of you. Now, allow the symbol to become one with your body with the cross in your heart chakra. Notice that all the knowledge you seek regarding your past or the future is within you. There is no need to look outside for it. Your lower three chakras store the energy of the past, and the upper three chakras have the energy of the future. The fourth chakra alone is the energy of the present time. (Energy in your symbol moves from left to right because the left side of the body receives the energy, and the right side sends out the energy.)

Another thing we want you to notice is that there is no equal time between the three of them. The present time is only a dot, cross, junction, and the tiniest moment of now. Yet, the present time is the only time from which the past can be healed and the future can be altered. Furthermore, the past predestines the future. To change the future, you need to heal your timelines while sailing on the boat of destiny and be aware that each action has an equal reaction.

ANCIENT PROPHECIES

The ancients left you prophecies. Some of them are warning prophecies. It is not to scare you or mentally prepare you for doomsday but to see what you could CHANGE based on these predicted events.

When someone is allowed to see into the possible future and share that information with others, this individual has been gifted by destiny with the ability to send messages into the future (from the present time) to allow you to change that future. There is no other reason than that.

Suppose the Earth should end by a particular day, and there is no chance of survival or altering the event. In that case, there is no need to know about it because mass hysteria does not serve any purpose for the Universe or any beings (whether they are of Light or Dark origin).

When the individual predicts several events and some materialize, there is solid proof that those unfulfilled predictions for the future are heading toward possible materialization. You still have time to change the outcome.

Think about it, (for example) someone with credible premonition skills warns you that tomorrow you should not walk on Main Street because you could get hit by a car and die. You always have a choice when making your decision. You can listen to the advice or ignore it and take your chances. In our example, you listened to the advice and avoided Main Street. That evening, while watching the news, you heard about a car accident on Main Street. This affirmed that it could have been fatal if you had been on Main Street. If something like this happens, it means that you were not destined to die on that day and that the Universe gave you a choice. The outcome of your choice became part of your new destiny. Therefore, based on your choice, you are at a new beginning in your life.

In the other example, you have a good friend with whom you practice energy healing, and she unexpectedly passes away a few days after you both shared the most magnificent session. You are flabbergasted, feeling guilty, because you did not feel anything wrong, yet she passed away suddenly. Why was there no warning? Why did you not sense anything? Why could you not save her?

You did not sense anything because her soul was at peace with passing (whichever way it happened) and ready for a new journey behind the veil. Her soul did not want to be alarmed because that would cause hysteria for something divinely planned by one's destiny and could not be changed. There was no need to know about it consciously ahead of time because it could not be changed.

Looking back at the ancient prophecies, the only reason they survived and are still on record is that you must take appropriate actions toward change, not to sit and wait for doomsday.

HEALING TIMELINES STARTS WITH YOU

The present time is the doorway into the past and the future. You can heal all your soul wounds from here. Learning to stay present in your mind, body, and soul is challenging but doable. Practice staying still and present in your heart, your fourth chakra. Your present time becomes zero-point energy, which means it has no energy/emotional charge. It has no wants, needs, emotional pain, excitement, or grudges; it just simply is. In neutral energy, you can see or sense the truth with your mind's eye for what it really is, and thus, you can send unconditional love to anyone without judgment. Currently, there is no blame, hurt, or fear. If you strive to stay in the present, you can distinguish between what you see with your physical eyes (what the world wants you to see) and the absolute truth you can perceive with your mind's eye. The next undertaking is to accept life as it is (surrender) and become a Temple of the Truth. The Temple of Truth means that you are a living embodiment of the truth and that all your actions are based on honesty and integrity.

This could be challenging. The human ego is conditioned to lie, twist the truth, and manipulate others, even if for excellent and honorable reasons. It is a habit, a pattern that helps one to survive. When you become a Temple of the Truth, you must recognize this pattern within you and overcome this human conditioning by striving to be true to yourself and others. This does not change overnight; it becomes a way of life the more you practice. Simply put, when you make a mistake, and your human self gets the better of you, do not blame others for your wrongdoing. Stop. Acknowledge and accept what happened so you can see the truth as to why you were behaving in that manner. The gift that will arise from this subtle, yet powerful change is the ability to see your past or past lives with new clarity, and they may need some profound healing. Only when you realize that you are broken can you heal.

When you feel upset, sad, angry, anxious, etc., over something, ask yourself, "What am I afraid of? What is the root of this feeling?" Allow yourself to be guided to this moment. Imagine that you are your own guardian angel, your higher self, and you know what you need to hear at that moment to help yourself feel better. Work with acceptance because acceptance enables you to see the truth behind your feelings or the motives of others. You cannot change what has happened, but you can surround yourself (in the past) with unconditional love, and you can change how you feel about it.

The next step is to apologize and forgive yourself (and others if needed), but before you do that, observe how much you trust yourself and others. If you have a trust issue, where did it originate from? Was it in this lifetime or another? What is the story behind it? Have you been abandoned or betrayed, and did this lead to your distrust in people, humanity, perhaps even the Universe, or God? Once again, the realization will open a new healing pathway. Forgiveness helps you to trust yourself and others. It will allow you to collect back the missing pieces of your immortal soul. It ends that event right there, and then there is no need to repeat it in the future. The energy imprint of that trauma will be gone, and you will never attract it again. Right there, you altered your future.

Last, fill yourself (and others) with unconditional love. You are the only one who has to like, love, and live with you; what others think about you is irrelevant. Self-love means valuing your energy, feeling worthy, being kind, and taking care of your mind, body, and spirit, ensuring that they are all healthy so you can serve others. Being in service is sharing unconditional love.

See, you are NOT wiping out the past but transforming unhealed energy into healed energy. A dysfunctional pattern into a supportive, successful pattern. Healing the past is acknowledging all life's lessons that provide you with knowledge and wisdom. The sun rises from the darkness, and life lessons are learned from suffering. When the soul registers the lesson and can accept and forgive, unconditional love is the only energy to replace suffering. The future that is projected from this energy is what you would like. It is the law of cause and effect, of sowing and reaping. The higher self will happily release the soul's memory to you to be in service. When ready, you can consciously exit the time loop and never return to Earth.

There are infinite possibilities for healing your timelines and projecting the possible future. The future could be projected only with unconditional love because unconditional love does not control the outcome. It does not have the wants and needs that humans have. It is aligned with destiny, yours, and Earth's. And the truth thrives in the unconditional love. This is a way of life, not a temporary adjustment.

This simple shift within yourself will lead to an incredible transformation in your life. Transformation is sometimes painful or bittersweet because giving up the old self is hard. Sometimes, you may get caught up in unpleasant situations. This is not because someone or something is trying to ruin your life, but you can master this ancient lesson. In the old days, you attended mystery schools. These days, the mystery school curriculum is woven into your everyday life when you ask for it.

You are a Reality Writer.
You are a Time Traveler.
You are a Magician.

TIME TRAVELING EXERCISE

Cultivate your time-traveling skills by consciously moving between two days of energy and stretching it into more days until you reach past lives as far back as you like. Dedicate the exact time each day to this practice. Repetition is the key.

Exercise:
1. Upon awakening in the morning, center yourself within your heart. Rest your hands over your heart chakra and focus only on your breath for a few seconds.
2. Then put your hands over your lower belly and talk with yourself about yesterday. This means you are talking to yourself, who was doing the same exercise yesterday morning. (Consistency is a key.) Trust yourself that this works. You know that you were lying here yesterday, doing the same things. Tell yourself about yesterday's events from today's morning's perspective. Tell yourself good things that will happen and prepare yourself for the bad that may occur. If you were upset over something, allow yourself to accept it, forgive, and send unconditional love to this particular incident. Be your guardian angel and share all you need to know (from yesterday) about the day ahead.
3. When you feel you are done, put your hands on your forehead, relax, and allow yourself to sense/feel/hear guidance for the day from your future self (tomorrow). If you have any questions about your day, simply ask. If

you need assistance with something, ask your future self for help.

In summary, focus on the heart chakra for the present moment. Send feedback about yesterday to your lower three chakras and receive guidance from the future in your upper three chakras. It is a sending-receiving, action-reaction process.

You may not feel any significant change when you try this exercise for the first time. However, with more practice, you'll be able to master it. Just like learning to ride a bike, it takes time and practice to gain confidence and make it feel natural. But eventually, it will become second nature to you.

Here is one example: Today, you have to give a speech in front of several people and feel nervous about it. Upon awakening in the morning, you check with your future self on how the speech went. Just breathe out your worries and expectations and ask. You will most likely feel the energy of a warm embrace and calmness and know you got this. This means your speech went well. You will be calm and confident when you give this speech because you (already) know it went well.

Now, let us speculate that your speech was terrible, and instead of feeling good, you get the urge and feel guided to rewrite it. If you follow your intuition, trust the guidance, and rewrite your speech, you are altering your future immediately, and your speech may come out better than expected.

The above exercise is just energy practice on moving between yesterday and today. Not everything can be changed to result in a positive outcome, but how you feel about it can be changed. When YOU change within, you are changing your future. You can develop a beautiful relationship with your past, present, and future selves based on mutual trust.

Once you practice this for a while, you can then experiment with connecting to your future self and asking questions about what it needs that you may be able to assist with - "How can I be in service to the future today, a day from now, a week from now, or even a hundred years from now?" "What is it that people in the future need so their life is peaceful and filled with love?" Your future self is aligned with your higher self; thus, the guidance on what you can create or contribute is aligned with the highest energy of destiny.

Note: Your higher self gives you only positive inspiration on how to be in service to the future. If you receive negative guidance, you are not connecting with your higher self but are being deceived by some imposing low-vibration energy. Be careful of this, learn to discern the energy, and stay vigilant to remain on the right path.

Chapter 4

Willpower

Healing your timelines activates the highest possible energy for the future. Changing yourself within will manifest that future. ~ Pleiadians

Since the time ancient aliens accepted animal DNA to genetically modify their bodies in Atlantis, the ego and soul began to compete over the vessel. Later on, the same fight continued within the human vessel. Eventually, the ego forgot that it is connected to the Universal Mind and that the ego and the soul are equal creators. It plunged deeply into fear. (Let us remember that the ego's original program was to ensure survival on Earth.) No one likes to live in fear for long, so the ego figured out how to use fear to manipulate and control others because it believes that control leads to fearlessness. Fear walks hand in hand with pain and suffering. And when the pain becomes unbearable, you may end up standing on a metaphorical ledge about to end the journey that's only just begun.

Life is a precious gift for many reasons. While you are alive, in your vessel, you are a creator; you are God, and God is you. Your power is equal to that of the

Universal Mind and the Cosmic Love combined. You can do anything or be anyone you wish to be.

On a subconscious level, the ego and soul know about their ongoing power struggle. They use your body as a puppet until YOU learn to be present and in charge of your life. When your suffering reaches your breaking point, the ego steps back and allows your soul to shine down upon you to give you the necessary love that will enable you to go on in your physical life. This is because the ego does not desire to actually end your journey through suffering. Believe it or not, the ego needs the soul, as the soul gives animation to the body. The soul needs the ego, as it makes the body intelligent and creates in the physical realm.

LEFT BRAIN VS. RIGHT BRAIN

Some star-seeds feel more vital in the left brain (ego energy) and thrive with intelligent technology. They desire to create inventions in all fields, from simple household gadgets to technology and medicine, that could help humankind. However, they need to be more open to connecting with the soul. They sometimes lack emotional, empathetic, and social skills. They believe that embracing love from within is nonsense. Their opinions are usually substantial. Unfortunately, some of their fantastic work may accidentally turn into a force of destruction (or self-destruction) as it lacks the component of love.

Other star-seeds feel more vital in the right brain (soul energy). They live from the heart, promote an organic way of life, and work hard to prove that holistic healing can help mankind. They are authentic and promote free will choices. Some struggle financially, and some are a bit eccentric. Often, they reject modern technology, modern-day medicine, and futuristic lifestyles and slowly separate themselves from others. They tend to be stubborn and refuse to negotiate with those not like them; thus, their excellent healing work is deemed charlatan or undiscovered. They fear that intelligent technology will control us all.

Each side is trying to convince the other that they are correct and that the good of the future depends on embracing their particular point of view. Each one lives in fear and thrives from suffering. Each believes their way of life is the only way to ensure a better future. However, one may only exist with the other, even though they may often reject each other.

Does this remind you of something? Does it remind you of stories of the twin flame love? One cannot function without the other. The ego and soul are stuck in a love/hate relationship, and each wants to change the other to become like him/her. They both have so many wants, needs, whining, and suffering. Yet each is throwing its own temper tantrum and unwilling to accept the other the way he/she is. The ego and soul have many reasons why the other should change.

From Suffering to Unconditional Love

Actual change starts with accepting the intelligent ego and the infinite soul as equal partners and evaluating the willpower you are currently using.

Willpower is an engine in your body. When your engine is off, you are in limbo, developing many problems that keep you stagnant, such as fear, frustration, and depression. There are only two sources to start your engine: the ego and the soul. The ego prefers fuel derived from suffering, while the soul prefers fuel derived from unconditional love.

The old mind program suggests that your creative will is activated by human suffering and that you grow from suffering. Your mind is designed to be trapped in the past. This means that it constantly swims in the torturing emotions of what has happened to you in this lifetime, with the excuse of trying to figure out how to heal it. To make things more interesting, once you start spiritually growing, your mind plunges into past lives so you can experience even more unresolved emotions. Notice that you are not often reminded about happy past lives, and instead, your mind is walking you through unresolved emotions without providing real solutions to heal them. If that is happening to you, something needs to change, as your mind is dangling a carrot of hope without a natural solution to keep you believing in it rather than helping you believe in yourself. The mind does not want you to figure out that you are an extraterrestrial being living in a human body. It does not want you to know that you have already endured several human lifetimes in which you were conscious about who or what you are. It does not want you to know that you are a creator.

For this reason, it keeps you in a loop: When you conclude that you are done with suffering, your willpower rises like wildfire, and you are inspired to change your life. You hover in dreamy clouds of the future where everything is possible and feel invincible. This may last for a few hours or days. Then, a memory of failure from your past (or from a past life) rekindles feelings of fear, anger, or frustration (because you cannot control everything and could possibly fail), and you question your actions. The steps you should take to change your life slowly dissipate, and you continue to live in the old mind program, fearing the possibility of failure.

Fear motivates survival.
Suffering influences creative willpower.
You create to survive.

There are many mind programs, which we call life patterns (rich, poor, healthy, sick, happy, spiritual, religious, fanatic, etc), that your mind will let you choose from. Your mind will support you in this decision, although it will also try to convince you that suffering is necessary for your life. Do not let this phase fool you, "I am grateful for all the suffering that I have experienced because it has made me into the person that I am today." While suffering is a humble and essential step in one's evolution, you should not continue to suffer after your evolution. You might have changed your pattern, and your life may be significantly better, but if your growth stems from suffering (as the human body is designed to), you are not a creator of your future. Something else may be running your life with the energy of suffering, as it is creative negative willpower.

Notice that you need a will to change or do anything. Will is the power that helps you move from one part of your life to another. To become a reality writer and change your life, you need willpower not linked to suffering. This new willpower is unconditional love.

Unconditional love willpower is activated by making a conscious connection with your soul and learning how to create with it. Humans do not naturally choose love as their willpower fuel because suffering is louder than love. The ego is your protector, as it has been for thousands of years. Love has to be consciously chosen by free will.

We hear you now, "Why do you have to embrace unconditional love as the new willpower?"

This is because if you reach a level of happiness without entirely and completely understanding love, that happiness will not last and will only be temporary. You will experience a crash toward low energy as soon as your happiness state peaks. This is why you experience highs and lows and are stuck in suffering. Reaching the happiness level without understanding love is like knowing the final answer to a math problem without knowing how you got it. Mistakes can be painful if you are about to face a similar situation without knowing the steps to take to solve it. After you learn to utilize unconditional love as your willpower, you can reach a state of nirvana and may choose to stay there. However, the nirvana state is just a state of being while holding this enlightening frequency for others; it is not creative and does not have the willpower or a magnificent state of being.

SUFFERING WILLPOWER VS. UNCONDITIONAL LOVE WILLOWER

Suffering Willpower	Unconditional Love Willower
fear motivates survival	love heal fears
suffering influences creative willpower	love influences creative willpower
you create to survive	you create to thrive and to be in service to others

EXCHANGE

Something interesting happens when you consciously grow from unconditional love rather than suffering. You will notice unmistakable signs, such as synchronicities, being guided to the right books, and being guided to new people and friends to help you on this journey. This happens because you are in sync with the cosmic energies. You will also notice that your beautiful ego, soul, and body trio will likely experience challenges and difficulties as they are used to suffering instead of love. Embracing new willpower is like entering unknown territory for the human body, yet it is a natural state for extraterrestrial beings (like yourselves).

Your mind, which is connected to your ego, will want to distract you from being consciously present in embracing love, feeling love, and being loved because it knows it could lose its control over you. It is afraid it will not be able to protect you.

Your soul will remind you of past lives. You have to heal your soul from past soul-PTSD traumas, and you may find yourself experiencing them again to heal them. What happened on Earth has to be healed on Earth.

Your body needs to rewire your nervous system to support the ego and soul in transforming to new willpower. Your body's nervous system could malfunction, making you sick (physically or emotionally) and tired. This is because you are (metaphorically said) attempting to run a new program on an old computer system. You are trying to bring your extraterrestrial consciousness (soul memory) into the human body, and the body does not know what to do and is trying to reject it. Your current nervous system can only support the old program of fear. Notice that your nervous system is always present, the same as your heartbeat or any other organ that you have. None of your body's organs function in the past or the future energy. You reprogram your willpower from the present time.

NERVOUS SYSTEM

Your nervous system is much more than you think it is. Let us talk about this a little further. It is the communicator between the physical life and the spiritual unknown. It is your psychic antenna (receiver and transmitter) and is precious. In the body, the nervous system is a conductor of energy for the ego (intelligence) and the soul (emotional/spiritual). Imagine each (ego and soul) as a separate pulsating electrical current. As a conductor, the nervous system combines these two currents into one that will work in harmony within the body. When they are out of balance, the pulse is separated into two different pulses, which may cause havoc in the physical body's organs and lead to physical diseases or psychological issues.

Many star-seeds have been born with weak nervous systems because they are trying to bring a more significant part of their soul consciousness into their human body. Challenges or weaknesses push you to evolve and upgrade the nervous system and integrate a higher level of consciousness. The human body is not capable of holding this energy without proper adjustments. Your nervous system is also weakened through life circumstances. Therefore, it needs to be adjusted.

A particular energy pathway within the nervous system is significant. It involves a connection between the second and sixth chakras carried through the body's organs (later, we will teach you an energy exercise that will work with this pathway). The bladder and digestive systems are critical to the nervous system in your body.

The bladder has its own electromagnetic field and can communicate with the whole body by sending out electric impulses. Your intuitive gut feeling occurs in the lower belly, not the stomach. This is your innate energy. This energy constantly regulates organ functions, even when someone is paralyzed or in a coma.

Next, look at the following two meridians, the Central meridian and the Governing meridian. Their pathways are the same as your central nervous system. Unlike the other 12 main meridians, these two are not assigned to any specific group of organs. They work as assistants to your nervous system. Your Central meridian starts at your pubic bone and ends at your bottom lip. Your Governing meridian begins at the bottom of your spine and continues over your head to your top lip. Hermes' symbol, Caduceus, depicts the connection between these two meridians and your central nervous system. Two serpents represent these meridians, and the winged staff represents the central nervous system. All of the three objects are interconnected. This symbol may also be interpreted as the ego and the soul (the two serpents) twining around the body–its nervous system (the winged staff).

The bladder, heart, and brain are directly connected through the Governing and Central meridian. These meridians keep circulating the energy information into the organs and the central nervous system. They serve as telephone lines. Each of these named organs (heart, bladder, brain) has its own electromagnetic field directly connected to the Vagus nerve, the longest nerve in your central nervous system. The Vagus nerve is the primary conductor of spiritual energy within the body. The Yogis called the Vagus nerve a Kundalini serpent.

Your bladder can communicate with your body in a language that can influence reprogramming. Your heart is the seat for your soul. It is also connected to Cosmic Love, can connect with the energy of oneness, and jumpstart the healing process within your body. Your brain speaks the language of your ego and can connect to the Universal Mind, allowing access to all of the universal knowledge. However, they must all work together to make anything transformative happen.

Your nervous system can access all past life traumas, as it can read and decode your DNA information. Your skeletal system is wired along with the nervous system. Bone marrow produces blood cells that carry energy information into the whole body. This enables you to reprogram your life patterns by replacing old and irrelevant information with new information.

The Essenes fully understood how to work with their physical nervous systems. Before their deaths, they intentionally energized their skeletons with the highest vibrational energy of their soul. After their soul left, their bodies were buried in the Earth (not cremated), and their bones would vibrate the particular frequency that they embodied. For example, unconditional love, ancient knowledge, wisdom, joy, happiness, or peace. It is well known that bones can be buried for thousands of years before they fully decay.

The Christ consciousness is literary buried inside the Earth in the bones of the Essenes.

In conclusion, suffering, addiction, exhaustion, poor diet, etc., can weaken your nervous system. Every illness sprouts from the weakened nervous system. Immunity disorders are the result of a compromised nervous system. The nervous system is your powerhouse that secures your body's good and healthy function. It also works as your spiritual antenna, particularly the Vagus nerve. It is the receiver and the transmitter of your soul memory. This nerve connects the ego's and the soul's energy to communicate with you through your body through emotions or physical pain until you learn to speak in the language of love.

A healthy diet, avoidance of substances, taking vitamins and minerals, Kundalini yoga, Kriya yoga, Pranayama breathing exercises, and many more are great physical tools for building up your nervous system.

Your emotional tools include positive thinking, meditation, learning ancient knowledge, eliminating fears, and embracing love.

ENERGY EXERCISES

We will share three energy exercises to help you become a reality writer. Each exercise builds upon the previous one. The first energy exercise is to connect with your nervous system and learn to communicate with your body. The second is to connect with your willpower, and the third concludes the process and guides you in manifestation.

Exercise 1 of 3

I Am Present

Holding your focus on the present time connects you with your body through your nervous system so you can establish communication with it.

1. Put your left hand on your urinary bladder (second chakra) **and your right hand on your mind's eye** (sixth chakra). Take a deep breath in and let it slowly out. Focus on your breathing. You are in the energy of now. Imagine that your auric field is filled with a blue color (any hue of blue you like). This is your blue energy healing ray. Take three slow and deep breaths and breathe this color in. Stay in the moment, focus on your breathing and the essence of blue. Continue with slow breaths and become one with the blue. It may help to imagine that your whole body is blue in color. Notice how it feels to be present in your body.

If you are having trouble quieting your mind, focus on your breathing. Focus on the sound you make while inhaling and exhaling. Now is not the time to resolve your thoughts or to be distracted by them. Focus only on your breathing. You should stay like this for 3-10 minutes. Once your energy connects between the second and sixth chakras, you will feel connected. You may suddenly have an urge to take a deep breath, which completes this step.

2. You can end with step one or **continue communicating with your body's nervous system**. Start with a simple yes/no question using answering techniques like the body pendulum or kinesiology testing.

For example:

- Are you overactive? (stressed out, anxious – need to find a way to distress and relax)

- Are you underactive? (suppressed – could be due to medication suppressing your abilities, exhaustion, malnutrition, poor diet, etc. If that is the cause, do your research, look into alternative choices, and talk to your medical professional provider.)

- Are you deficient? (Most star-seeds suffer from mineral deficiency, and their nervous systems are in havoc. They think they have a wide range of awakening symptoms, whereas, in reality, they just have a mineral deficiency, which is depleting their nervous system. If this is true, they usually feel better within three days after corrective measures are taken.)

Those are just a few examples. You can ask any questions.

Exercise part 2 of 3

Choosing Unconditional Love for Willpower

In this energy exercise, you will first connect with your body and experience how it feels to be in the present time (as instructed in part 1). Next, you will mentally connect with your ego and acknowledge the energy of suffering. There is nothing to be afraid of. It is just energy that needs to be understood. You will then tune into your soul and ask to feel the willpower of unconditional love. If you resonate with this new willpower, you can choose it as a new program. Do not rush through this; take your time with it. This exercise is about being aware of both willpowers, distinguishing between those energies, and being mindful that you have a choice as to which one you will embrace.

1. Invocation

Say aloud or in your mind, *"I ask and thank you to be connected to the highest energy of God, my higher self, to the frequency of unconditional love. I ask you to bring unconditional love into my whole body."* Imagine that your body, starting at your head and continuing down to your toes, is filled with this beautiful energy.

2. I am in the present

Once again, put your left hand on your bladder (second chakra) and your right hand on your mind's eye (sixth chakra). Take a deep breath in and let it slowly out. Focus on your breathing. You are in the energy of now. Imagine that your auric field is filled with a blue color (any hue of blue you like). This is your blue energy healing ray. Take three slow and deep breaths and breathe this color in. Stay in the moment, focus on your breathing and the essence of blue. Continue with slow breaths and become one with the blue. It may help to imagine that your whole body is blue in color. Notice how it feels to be present in your body.

3. Ego

Next, put your left hand over your liver area and your right hand over your right hip or leg. Imagine that your auric field is filled with a red color (any hue of red you like). This is your red energy healing ray. Take three slow, full breaths and breathe this color in. Stay in the moment, focus on your breathing and the essence of red. It may help to imagine that your whole body is red in color. Continue with slow breaths and become one with red.

Acknowledge your ego and engage in conversation, *"Hello, my ego. I am happy to connect with you. I love you. I am aware of how much you suffered. I know how suffering empowered us (you and me) and protected us. I know you mean well for us."*

Allow yourself to feel a time when you truly suffered—when you were sick, had a difficult time, or felt cornered in darkness. Feel how desperate it felt and become aware of how your ego supplied you with the willpower to survive. Express your gratitude: *"I am grateful for your help."*

Next, focus on the present again, focus on your breathing, and keep talking to your ego, *"Would you like to stop this suffering? Are you willing to change? Would you be willing to work together as friends with the soul and find love and happiness?"*

49

Now, bring your awareness into your mind and invite your ego to join you there. *"Follow me, my ego, I want to show you something. I ask and thank you to be connected with the Universal Mind."* Feel the rush of intelligent energy coming into your mind. Focus on your breathing and feel the connection to the source of all universal knowledge.

"Dear ego, when you are, I am ready to see the past lives we need to heal to access this universal knowledge. I am ready, when you are, to embrace unconditional love as our new willpower and to access ancient knowledge on healing, inventions, technology, thriving, and other things. Are you willing to work with the divine soul to connect with the Universal Mind and share this knowledge with humanity?"

Take your time.

4. Soul

Next, put your right hand on your spleen area and your left hand on your head. Imagine that your auric field is filled with a green color (any hue of green you like). This is your green energy healing ray. Take three slow, full breaths and breathe this color in. Stay in the moment, focus on your breathing and the essence of green. It may help to imagine that your whole body is green in color. Continue with slow breaths and become one with green.

Acknowledge your soul and engage in conversation, *"Hello, my soul. I am happy to connect with you. I love you."* Take time to enjoy all you perceive.

Next, connect your soul to your ego, *"Can you please become friends with my ego?"*

Focus on your breathing and imagine that your soul is meeting your ego and that they like each other. Now it is time to connect to Cosmic Love. *"I ask and thank you for my soul and ego being connected to Cosmic Love."* Allow yourself to bask in your soul family's warm rays of love.

"I am ready to surrender. I am ready to let go of my control, fear, and desire as I let you, my higher self, my soul's family, and God's consciousness guide me on this journey. I am willing to accept unconditional love as my creative willpower."

Allow yourself to enjoy this profound feeling.

5. Record your new willpower in your nervous system.

Return back to your nervous system. Put your left hand on your urinary bladder (second chakra) and your right hand on your mind's eye (sixth chakra). Take a slow and full breath in and out. Focus simply on your breathing. Imagine that your auric field is filled with a blue color (any hue of blue you like).

Notice how it feels to be back present in your body while consciously aware of your soul and ego energy. Accept both as your sister and brother who thrive from unconditional love. From now on, you are family. Your ego and soul are one in the body.

Repeat this exercise often until you feel energetically connected to your ego, soul, and body.

Manifesting Your New Life with Knowing and Feeling

knowing + feeling = manifesting

Before proceeding to the third part of this exercise, we want you to be aware of two important factors: knowing and feeling.

Knowing (the ego's energy): Think of the idea you want to manifest. When brainstorming your idea, set the intention that what you create is aligned with honesty and integrity and is in service to humanity. Know what you want.

Feeling (the soul's energy): Bring the soul's emotions into your idea. Fill your idea, your dream, with unconditional love and allow yourself to imagine how you would feel when your idea becomes reality. Next, bring all these emotional feelings into your second chakra (your bladder). Experience all the emotional details of it, how it felt when you received it.

Manifesting (the body's energy) - You must bring your knowing and emotional feelings into your nervous system through your central two conscious receptors – the second and sixth chakra (bladder and brain). When these two energies connect, they project the energy you just created into your auric field so you can attract what you are seeking. In this projected energy, what you want to be manifested is a done deal.

Exercise part 3 of 3

Manifesting

In this exercise, you will invite your ego and soul to participate actively. Choose unconditional love as your willpower for this project and record it in your nervous system so that your nervous system can project it into your auric field. All you have to do afterward is pay attention to signs and synchronicities in your life and follow your soul's guidance (your higher self) instead of doing it your way. Trust the process and believe in yourself.

1. Invocation

Say aloud or in your mind, *"I ask and thank you to be connected to the highest energy of God, my higher self, to the frequency of unconditional love. I ask you to bring unconditional love into my whole body."* Imagine that your body, starting at your head and continuing down to your toes, is filled with this beautiful energy.

2. Know what you want

Next, put your left hand over your liver area and your right hand over your right hip or leg. Imagine that your auric field is filled with a red color (any hue of red you like). Take three slow, full breaths and breathe this color in and out. Stay in the moment, focus on your breathing and the essence of red. Continue with slow breaths and become one with red. You can even imagine that your whole body is red in color.

Connect with your ego and share what you want to manifest (create your own words; this is just an example). *"Dear ego, I want us to write a book. Would you please help me connect to all the ancient knowledge and lives we had on Earth so we can share their wisdom? I want us to connect to the Universal Mind with all the writers who want to assist us in this project. Will you please allow for the soul to guide us on this journey? Thank you. Thank you. Thank you."*

Give your ego time to fully connect with your idea of what you want to manifest.

3. Feel what you want

Next, put your right hand on your spleen area and your left hand on your head. Imagine that your auric field is filled with a green color (any hue of green you like). Take three slow, full breaths and breathe this color in. Stay in the moment, focus on your breathing and the essence of green. Continue with slow breaths and become one with green. You can even imagine that your whole body is green in color.

Connect with your soul: *"Dear soul, I want to write a book that will assist humanity in creating a better life. Will you please guide me on this journey? I want to be connected to Cosmic Love, and I chose the source of unconditional love as my willpower for this project. Thank you. Thank you. Thank you."*

Bring the soul's emotions into your idea. Fill your idea and dream with unconditional love, and allow yourself to imagine how you will feel when your idea becomes reality. Feel it like it had already happened.

4. Record it in your nervous system

Put your left hand on your bladder (second chakra) and your right hand on your mind's eye (sixth chakra). Take a slow and full breath in and out. Focus on your breathing. Imagine that your auric field is filled with a blue color (any hue of blue you like).

You know what you want in your mind and how it feels when you manifest it. Keep your hands on your nervous system receptors while you indulge in this fantasy. Your ego and soul agreed to assist you and are madly in love with your request and with you. Bring this feeling into what you ask for, and employ all your senses to make your future dream a present fact.

Hold this energy of knowing, feeling, and love for approximately three minutes or until you feel the energy clicked and are done. Express gratitude to your ego, soul, body, Earth, Universe, and soul family. *Thank you. Thank you.* Thank you for assisting me. Then, go about your day.

CHAPTER 5

MATCH MADE IN HEAVEN

This parable is about the Twin Flame relationship of the ego and the soul.

Once upon a time, there was a handsome man named Ego. Ego grew up as an orphan who did not know who his parents were. Ego had an agile mind, was a skilled hunter and survivor, and went through life without attracting too much attention to himself. His masculine, solid arms were precise with any tools or weapons. His deep eyes held an ancient wisdom. The worry lines across his forehead told stories of sadness, pain, and suffering. Fortunately, the wrinkles around his eyes revealed that he could find humor in his life. They showed that he was forgiving and kind. Ego walked in the shadows of the Earth. He was lonely and tired. He wished to walk out of the darkness and into the sunlight. He overheard stories about the beauty of the blossoming flowers. He silently wondered why he could not remember them.

There were many others in Ego's tribe, males and females. However, one needed a partner from the other side to venture out of the shadows and into the sunlight.

Some tried to disobey this rule but were caught and gruesomely punished. They had to wait until their partner signaled to meet in a physical form (a vessel). Patience, unfortunately, was not the best virtue of his tribe, Ego thought, with a smirk on his face.

Soul lived in the heavenly realms. Her face was radiant, without any wrinkles. She knew Ego very well. Soul's beauty shined from the inside out. Her kindness touched the hearts and souls of everyone around her. Soul smiled, thinking about how many times she had been married to Ego when she was on Earth. She knew that the Earth had made him forget about her each time she had left the union of the body they shared. She shook her head as a deep sigh escaped from her mouth. She worked hard to remind him of who she was every time they met. It was a pity that he was not allowed to remember her. This time, she was ready for another incarnation on Earth and vowed it would be different.

Once again, the Eternal Flame ignited, deeming Ego and Soul ready to meet again.

When his eyes met with hers, for what he thought was the first time, he felt like he could not breathe. He wondered, have they met before? Impossible, he thought. How could someone not remember her? Yet there was something about her. Instantly, her presence soothed his pain, and even his mind quieted down. It was like she held some kind of magic, he thought.

"Nice to meet you, Ego." Her voice chimed as she stood on her tippy toes and gently kissed his cheek. Ego did not know what to do. The kiss completely ungrounded him. They should be strangers, yet she is acting like she has always known him. On one hand, he felt rejuvenated. On the other, he was greatly perplexed. After all, he was an abandoned orphan. He believed that his parents had given up on him because he was not good enough for them. He thought that he was not worthy of her kindness and generosity. Does she not see it? Is this not obvious to everyone? He believed that this must be some kind of heavenly mistake. How could the divine source send him this angel?

Ego was speechless. If this was a heavenly mistake and she was meant to meet someone else, he should tell her right away. However, he could not help himself. He simply gazed into her mesmerizing eyes. Despite his inner turmoil, Ego could not control his feelings and instantly fell in love. Did she bewitch him? Right there, he decided he would pretend to be someone else for whom she had mistaken him. Maybe she would never find out, he hoped.

Soul smiled and said softly under her breath, "You have not changed a bit."

"Excuse me?" the sound of her voice brought him out of his inner turmoil.

"I am glad we are finally meeting," she answered with sweet politeness.

Soul was secretly happy to be reunited again. Ego wanted to impress her rather than reveal he fell madly in love with her at first sight. He instantly feared that she would one day find out he was not the one for her. He was worried that if she realized who he was or what he believed himself to be, she would never love him or be able to look him in the eyes with that pure innocence she held.

He wanted her to love him. It hurt inside how much he wanted that. Ego viewed Soul as a fragile being. How could she survive the harshness of Earth's life if he did not protect her? At that exact moment, he made it his sole life purpose to defend her by all means. He swore to himself that he would do anything, anything, to protect her survival, even if it meant extreme suffering for him. He was her devoted servant, and his love for her was so possessive that he would lock her in a golden cage to keep her safe rather than give her freedom to shine her beautiful presence on everyone else. Ego knew what a cold world the Earth could be, how cruel humans are, and the levels of suffering one must endure. He never wanted Soul to experience this in its fullness. If he could spare Soul of all that suffering, it would be the highest honor for him to uphold.

"Is everything all right with you? You look lost in your thoughts," Soul asked gently. She enjoyed her reunion with her fear-consumed warrior. She knew the steps he would take to seclude her from participating in life. She loved Ego unconditionally and knew she had to take small and careful steps to win over his trust.

"I, I was just thinking," said Ego.

"That you should take me for a walk?" she jumped in before he could finish. Ego nodded eagerly, "Yes." He knew he was broody and did not want to spoil the moment.

The time came and went. Ego and Soul spent much time talking, laughing, and falling in love. But whenever she invited him to visit her family, he would explain why he was not ready. They were connected, yet it felt like they were miles apart. She knew there were secrets he was hiding. It made her sad that he did not yet fully trust her.

Their romantic life was beautiful, but as time passed, Soul worried that she did not have a voice to speak. She felt like Ego expected her to be content and happy living in the golden cage he had built around her to keep her safe. Soul started to feel trapped. Whenever she tried to reason with Ego, Ego had a reasonable and logical explanation for why this was best. Every time she asked Ego to meet her family, he refused.

One day, Ego became terribly sick. He could not leave his bed, and to his dismay, he could not protect Soul by ordering her to do what she needed to do to stay safe. Stubborn as she was, Soul reached out to her soul family for help. They visited often, but Ego did not see them with his eyes. They stood by her and offered compassion. Ego met them only in his fever-induced sleep. In his dreams, he allowed himself to be nourished by the compassion of the loving family. It felt good to be part of a big family. He thought he was hallucinating, so he indulged in these visions. In his awakened state, his weakness forced him to accept help from Soul. He could sense that he was close to death, and he knew very well when one flame goes out, the other goes out as well. Their journey starts and ends together.

"I do not want anything to happen to you. I love you so much," Ego whispered.

She caressed his face and looked deeply into his tired eyes. "I love you." tears filled her eyes. She was worried that she might lose him, but she held onto every tiny piece of hope that this would not be the end. "Can you promise me something?" she asked with urgency.

"Anything," He replied weakly.

"Promise me that you will meet my family if you heal and recover."

"But..." Even on his deathbed, he was stubbornly reluctant, and she wondered why. Why did he not want to meet her family? Why was he being so difficult about that? The tears escaped her eyes and were falling uncontrollably.

Slowly, he raised his hand to touch her cheek, to comfort her. He knew that he was dying, but he could not bear to see her sad.

"If I make it through this, I will meet your family," he said in a whisper.

The shock of hearing him say this startled her. "Promise me!" she urged him. "Ego, promise me that you will meet my family!"

With the last bit of strength, he whispered, "I promise," then his consciousness swept away, his eyes closed, but his pulse was still beating. There was still hope, Soul thought.

She connected to her soul family and pleaded, "Dear soul family, I ask that you hear me today. I ask for your help to save Ego, please."

The beings of light almost instantly surrounded Soul and Ego, "Why would you like us to save him? What is your reason?"

"Because I love him," replied Soul.

The beings of light looked compassionately at Soul, "Human love is not a good enough reason. Human love comes and goes; you know this, Soul." They repeated again, "Why would you like us to save him? What is your reason?"

"Because I love him!" she yelled out, sobbing.

The beings of light extended their arms and created a pink energy field around Soul. "Our divine child, we love you unconditionally. You know that you can meet Ego in a human body again as many times and as many lifetimes as you would like to. But when his time is up, you will have to say goodbye and wait for another time when you will be reunited again. For us, time is irrelevant. A hundred years on Earth feels like a day for us. You are one of us. You know this. Why are you asking us this time to save him? What is your reason?"

Soul was able to calm down a little as she realized that her worries were clouding her mind. Her soul wounds from previous unions with Ego were resurfacing and causing her stress. She hoped that they would be able to heal a significant part of their lives together this time. Now, it seemed that time was running out. Remembering human suffering and all the painful deaths they shared, she felt like she was suffocating. She took a few slow, calming breaths, and suddenly, the sentence that her soul family kept repeating was echoing in her head. *Why would you like us to save him? What is your reason?* She knew they could grant her a wish. But only if she had a good enough reason. Suddenly, she remembered what the old book was saying. One has a reason to thrive if one pursues a higher mission to serve others.

"He is willing to change and meet you. He is willing to work on ascension, and his actions will inspire others like him." she blurted out quickly.

Everyone quieted down. The tension was almost unbearable. All eyes were looking at her.

"Once he is better, he will meet you, and you can teach him." she stood up confidently, drying her wet eyes and smoothing her hair.

"Are you aware, our child, that if you are wrong about this, you will suffer terrible consequences with him?"

"Yes, I am fully conscious of my choice."

A woman with a glowing aura, dressed in a light blue gown, stepped forward and gracefully moved her hands, creating several hand mudras. Light from her hands moved into Ego's abdomen. She laid one of her hands on his abdomen and the other on his forehead. She chanted in the Language of Light. When finished, she reached into her robe to pull a piece of paper.

"Soul here is a written herbal remedy taken from the Akashic records to heal Ego. Meditate with Mother

Earth and ask her to bless these herbs. Give these to him for seven days. He will fully recover. You have three months until we meet again. Remember that you cannot tell him we healed him. He has to meet us with his own free will."

"I am so grateful. Thank you." whispered Soul.

The beings of light disappeared as fast as they had appeared. Then, she was alone with Ego, who was now sleeping peacefully. She caressed his hair with unsteady hands. She tried to grasp that their fate had changed in a few minutes.

"I fought for you," she told him, knowing he could not hear her. "I never fight. I just wait and wait and wait for another lifetime, for another opportunity. But this time, I fought for us, and they came. They helped us." For a while, she just sat in silence and looked at him. Then she said, "I hope you will fight for us, too."

He stirred, startling her. "I will be right back with your medicine." She kissed him on the forehead and left.

In a week, Ego was cured. Everyone said it was a miracle.

"I do not understand what happened. One day, I was dying, and then something happened. I cannot recall what it was, but I started feeling better," Ego stated.

"Ego, do you remember the promise you made me?" Soul asked.

"Hmm?" Ego looked puzzled.

"You promised me that if you get better, you will meet my family," she said with a serious face.

"I do not remember that," he snapped. Did she not understand? He cannot meet her family. He is an impostor who stole their daughter from some fantastic guy who was waiting for her. How could he stand there and look them in the eyes?

"I was too sick to make any promises. Please, Soul, come here, let's not argue. I was so afraid I would lose you. I cannot bear to lose you," he said while hiding the truth that he remembered his promise to her.

"And I can? I should just be happy about it? Do you know how worried I was for you?"

Ego just stood there. He had never seen Soul upset. "Let's talk about it another time."

She nodded and walked to her room. The door closed, and Ego was alone. He sighed heavily. What should he do? He tried his best to protect, please, and make her happy, but it was not working well.

For two days, Soul would not leave her room. She locked herself in. First, he knocked. Then he pleaded. Then he threatened. Then he begged. He was angry. He yelled that he would break the door down, but nothing worked. Ego felt miserable and guilty.

"I think I am getting sick again!" he yelled out of hopelessness to get her to hear him.

On the third day, Soul left her room, looking pale and frail. "If you cannot meet my family, then that is fine. However, I cannot be your supportive wife anymore. I will be here until our time ends, and you do what you must accomplish in this lifetime. But from now on, it will be your solo mission. I will wait here for you like I have done before in so many lifetimes."

"What?" asked Ego. It was killing him to see her frail, her eyes red from crying. Yet no tears fell while she spoke. What had he done? "Soul, you do not understand."

"Oh, yes, I do." She said rather coldly.

"You are too afraid to meet family. You think you are not worthy, not good enough for me. You think you must keep hiding so that those who matter to me will never know you exist."

His breath was stuck in his lungs. Had she known all this time that he was an impostor? Before he could collect his thoughts, she continued.

"Why, Ego? Why does it always have to be your way? Why do you see me as a pretty, weak little thing? Am I just a lucky charm to you? That I would not survive without your constant protection?" she stood before him, "Why do you have to be so paranoid? Why does everything have to pose a fear?"

"You do not know this world!" he shouted. "You have not seen the things I have seen, the things I must protect you from. You think everything is just love and light, but you are wrong. This world is cruel. Suffering and fear keep us alive. You have to do what you have to do to survive!"

"What about love?" she interrupted impatiently.

Frustrated, he answered, "Love is rare in this place."

"But you found it, we found it. Did we not?"

The shame was like a sharp knife twisting in his belly; he had to tell her. She deserved the truth!

"I stole it!"

"You stole what?" she looked perplexed.

He sat down defeated, covered his face with his hands, and spoke slowly in an exhausted voice.

"I stole the love. I was not meant to be your husband in the first place. There must have been some heavenly mistake. Look at you, Soul; you are beautiful, intelligent, and kind-hearted. How in the world would heaven match you with me? I am a loser. I was given up for adoption shortly after my birth. My parents were not interested in me. I do not even know who they are. I lived in shady places and have done things I wish I could forget. When I first looked at you, I fell in love. You made me feel things I thought I was not capable of feeling. I did not want anyone else to be your husband, so I stole you for myself. I should have told you that this was a mistake. You were probably meant to meet someone else. I am sure you were meant to be matched with someone else who would give you all you deserve in this life."

"Hmm...what do I deserve, Ego?" she asked.

"Much more abundance than what I can give you. A pretty house, more money. Enough so you can visit all the places you always talk about."

"So, are you saying that if you were rich, from a reputable family, with the right upbringing, you would be more of a suitable husband for me? If you were all that, could you look my family in the eyes and feel good about yourself?"

"Yes," he said very slowly. Why did he feel that he was suddenly unsure of his answers? And... why was she so calm?

"And, what about love, Ego? What if this amazingly successful man did not love me?"

"Oh, he would love you," he stated with assurance.

"Really, would he love me like one of his possessions in his successful office? Would that be love with wants and needs and obsessions? Will I be the..." she paused for a moment, "the lucky one who would fulfill this man's demands?"

"I do not mean it that way." he said squeamishly.

"Tell me the truth!" she demanded. "Did you fall in love with me because you thought I was from the right family?"

"No."

"Then why did you instantly fall in love with me right there. Why?" she asked.

He swallowed, his voice almost inaudible, "I... I looked into your eyes, and there was something so familiar about you, so comforting. I felt like I knew you. You were a good friend I had not seen in a while. We could just catch up and continue where we left off last time. I do not even understand what I felt, Soul. I felt that I needed to be by your side forever. Even if I were not your loved one, I would settle simply to be your friend. When you showed affection to me, I was the happiest man alive. Soul, I respect you and want to protect you. I would die for you. I would do anything for you."

"Anything?"

"Yes, anything." he said with confidence in his voice.

"If I tell you I do not love you, would you let me go?"

He was quiet for a while, but then he spoke, "This is hard for me, and it would probably kill me, but you taught me that love is not about wants and needs. If I want you just for myself without considering your feelings, I would keep you trapped like a bird in a cage. And that is exactly what I have done to you. I am sorry. Can you ever forgive me? I know you were a sad bird. You are supposed to be free. You can go. I am sorry that I have trapped you with me."

"What are you saying, you foolish man?" her eyes widened.

"I know I forced my love on you. I was wrong. You are free now." he tried not to cry. The pain of imagining her leaving was nearly unbearable.

"You know, you have it all wrong. Your assumptions are astounding!"

"What?" he lifted his eyebrows.

She spoke again with a deep sigh and short yet dramatic pause, "I am positive you were the one I came here to be with. I am with you because I love you, not because I have to be with you. If I were to be here just for the matter of our union, I would spend all my time in my room and hardly interact with you. We definitely had a past life like that."

"What?" was all he could say.

"Never mind," she continued, "You are amazing, smart, kind, and inventive. You are my man, my hero, and my everything! You are worthy to be loved. You are worthy to be successful. You are worthy to fulfill all your wishes and dreams. I want to help you with all of that. I wish to be equal partners in all that we do."

"Really?" he asked excitedly.

She walked to him, and they embraced in the hug they both longed for.

"And Ego," she lifted her chin to look at him in his eyes. "My family is your family."

He hesitated a moment. "I will meet them," he finally said. The rest of their words were lost in a deep and passionate kiss.

A few days later, Ego and Soul met Soul's family. Ego was very nervous, but Soul was gleaming with happiness. "Do not worry; they will love you," she said. Ego just grounded his teeth. Guilt wrenched his stomach. It was literally eating him alive. Fearful thoughts dominated his mind, which in turn created paranoia. His body felt weak. If only all the emotions could just stop or freeze, he wished, for just one moment.

"Come on, Ego. What is the worst thing that could happen?" she asked, looking at his tormented face.

"They reject me, and you will realize your mistake."

"That is always a possibility," she grinned. "How would that make you feel, Ego?"

"Bad," he almost laughed with irony. "I guess I would have a good reason for the shame, guilt, fear, and anger I am feeling right now. I really wish I was someone better for you," he said truthfully.

"I love you, Ego; you have nothing to worry about."

Just then, a golden portal appeared in front of them. Ego tried to shield Soul with his body and pushed her behind him. "What is this?" he shouted frantically.

"Oh, Ego, do not worry. It is similar to an elevator that will take us to my family. There is nothing to worry about," she smiled.

"Huh?"

"Just come with me," she said, pulling his hand and body into the golden portal elevator. When the elevator stopped, and the door opened, they entered what Ego could only identify as a magical world.

She excitedly squeezed his hand when they arrived at the Twin Flame Temple. Ego was mentally prepared for all the possible worst-case scenarios. However, he was not prepared for what he saw. The temple was majestic, and his mind was spinning. Just then, the beings of light walked in. He had no time to think; everything was happening so fast, and he was positive that he was not on Earth. Was he just dreaming? He wondered.

"Welcome to the Twin Flame Temple, Soul and Ego. Please sit down and enjoy the refreshments prepared for this joyful event."

Soul sat down, but Ego just stood and stared in disbelief.

"You are real," he finally said.

"We see you recognize us. We are pleased about this."

"It was you. You healed me when I was sick. I thought I was just hallucinating, but it was you who saved my life. Thank you," he bowed in front of them. "I am eternally grateful to you," and he could not help but ask, "Are you, Gods?"

"Please sit down," they gestured with their hands, and Ego finally accepted their invitation.

"Meeting face to face awakened your memory. We are Soul's family, and we are your family as well. We love you dearly. By accepting to meet us, by your own free will, you are allowed to remember."

Ego was looking at them with amazement, while Soul just smiled. Maybe he is dreaming again, he thought. He pinched himself to awaken from this dream.

"We are as real as you are, Ego. You are a being of light who sacrificed his divinity to be anchored in the 3D realm of Earth. Soul is your twin flame. You join together in the body for each incarnation. You hold the animal 3D energy, and Soul holds the divine 5D energy. Your creative willpower is fueled by suffering. Soul's creative willpower is fueled by unconditional love. Every time the body ends its journey, you stay on Earth while Soul returns to us to rejuvenate. Your true parents are beings of light who anchored their energy in the Earth realm. Soul's mission is to assist you in finding love, not romantic or lusty, but unconditional love. This is so that you both can heal the wounds that these Earth lifetimes bestowed upon you. Once your wounds are healed, you can return here together.

Ego, we know that Earth makes you forget who you are. There is nothing we can do about that, but for now, in our presence, we can awaken all your memories. We can share with you all of your past lives with Soul to learn from them and heal them. When you heal your past, you will collect the missing pieces of your infinite Soul. These pieces hold the secrets of your authentic and original soul memory, your power. Is this something you would wish us to do?"

Everything they said made sense to Ego. "Yes."

"Close your eyes and breathe deeply," they directed energy into his mind's eye.

Suddenly, Ego felt as if he was in the presence of a great mind. The energy was unbelievable. He felt like he instantly knew the answer to every question. In his mind's eye, he could witness the Earth and human evolution from the beginning until now.

"You are in the presence of the Universal Mind. It is your birthright to be connected to this wealth of information. When you come back into your body, Soul and you will have to work in unity to reach this energy in fullness as you are doing right now. We have faith that you will master this ability."

Then they gestured toward Soul. "Now, Soul, please open your energy to allow Ego to connect fully with the Cosmic Love energy."

Soul put one of her hands on her heart and the other on Ego's heart and suggested he do the same. He did. "Look deeply into my eyes," she whispered.

Unexpectedly, Ego was filled with an overwhelming surge of love. He could not think. He experienced nirvana. Tears were spontaneously coming from the corners of his eyes, yet he was not aware that he was crying. He could sense his parents and their unconditional love for him. He felt love for everyone and everything, himself included. He sensed that everything was collectively connected and thrived from love. Even the Universal Mind thrived from this collective love. He understood that when one finds unconditional love, one would no longer want to be a part of any war or military conflict and never abuse knowledge attained from the Universal Mind. One would like to be in service and devote the rest of his time to assisting the other beings of light lost within the Earth realm.

His tears were falling quietly, but they were tears of joy and happiness, a symbol of love for all creation and understanding.

"Ego, you are not trapped in the Earth realm. Neither of you is. Can you see that now?"

"Yes, I can. Thank you for showing this to me," he said humbly.

"We thank you for taking the leap of faith, letting go of your Earth-limited beliefs, and trusting Soul."

"Why cannot everyone see this?" Ego asked.

"Everyone can meet us and gain knowledge. First, one must let go of one's preconceived beliefs and allow oneself to be led to this place. The same way you allowed Soul to lead you. One has to lose himself before one can find himself again. Before one can find his original self again, one must let go and let his higher self in."

"One cannot reach the Universal Mind before accepting unconditional love as your main creative power. Once in a while, we allow individuals to obtain particular information that would enable them to bring new inventions to mankind. We hope that humanity will use these inventions to create rather than destroy. Everything is subject to cause and effect. Your actions today will have a significant impact on yourself and others. Now, it is up to you to accept or reject it. The collective mission for Soul and you is still ongoing. You must return to the body and decide what is ahead of you.

If you choose to work with Soul and allow her to lead you, you can cultivate your abilities and regain your soul memory, not as an individual, but as an equal couple. You can be in service to humanity while doing any kind of work as long as you do it with unconditional love. You will work together to heal your past and grow together. Then, by the end of your life, you can return home together when your vessel and job are done. Or you can forget what happened here today and continue in an ordinary life without growth."

"I want this," Ego said with a calm mind.

"If this is your free will choice, then you are truly married to Soul. Let us make a record of it in your Book of Life. From today, Ego's mind and Soul's emotions will work in synchronicity. The body you are occupying can manifest anything you two desire. The choice is always yours. We would never order you to do something, but we will always support you in your highest endeavor."

"You are eternally blessed. You are loved unconditionally. You are supported by the whole Universe. Now it is time for you to go back."

"Will I remember all of this?" Ego asked suddenly.

"You will remember part of this. After all, you were quite scared of coming here."

"Yes, I was." Ego smiled.

"You will remember the important parts to get you started on this marvelous journey. Soul will assist you in regaining this memory. Work in balance and harmony together. Do not be afraid to experience both good and bad emotions. Observe them, understand them, learn from them, and grow from them. Be an example to others."

"Thank you," Ego and Soul said simultaneously.

"Ego," Soul touched his arm gently. Let me show you something before we return. "Do you see this triangle?" he nodded. This is our symbol, the symbol that triggers our memories when we are back in our bodies. You will always remember this symbol. I will make sure you will always remember this symbol."

"I will try to remember it, Soul. Thank you. Thank you for all you have done for me. I love you."

"I love you, too," replied Soul.

It was then time to return to their Earth body. Ego felt like he had an incredibly realistic dream and shared it with Soul when he woke up. Soul smiled and pointed to a birthmark on Ego's body in the shape of a triangle. Ego jumped with excitement, "It was not a dream! It was real. It was all real!"

Life took on a new meaning when Ego and Soul started working together on ascension and being in service while living happily in the body called (add your name). This is your story and your happily ever after.

CHAPTER 6

OPENING A FIELD OF INFINITE POSSIBILITIES

The Universe likes bold people. ~ Pleiadians

The conscious decision to change your life can open up endless possibilities. The mere thought of it can bring a ray of hope into your being, like the morning sun shining through a small opening in a dark cavern. This signifies a new beginning.

So far, you have learned the importance of accepting yourself as a beautiful synergy of the ego and soul. You have also learned to be present and communicate with your body, as well as to choose unconditional love as a means of creating your willpower. This unconditional love is essential to opening up a field of infinite possibilities while using suffering willpower for the same reason could lead to unpleasant outcomes.

Staying present in your life from now on and creating from this present time is the recipe for success. Remember, the Universe likes bold people. You need to be an active doer rather than a scaredy cat. The Universe does not have favorites for who it will welcome into the field and whom it will not. It all depends on you, your choices, and your perseverance. When you do your work, the doors automatically open for you.

NEW AFFIRMATIONS

When you are ready to play in the field of infinite possibilities, you will need new affirmations to remain stabilized in this new energy level. This is new for your body's nervous system and ego, as they used to thrive off of fear. Take your time to go over these new affirmations. Repeat them, believe them, and physically (as well as energetically) feel them. Understand that your 3D energy is expanding toward the 5D energy.

I am safe.
I have freedom.
I am in service to humanity.

DECISIONS AND EMOTIONS

The ego makes you often feel victimized by unfavorable circumstances that may have developed throughout your past and present lifetime. It is simpler for the ego to keep you afraid, victimized, or angry rather than reveal your unique natural ability to plan and organize your life and make decisions based on your choices. These abilities are reflected within your organs, which was well documented in ancient Eastern medicine. The body holds all the answers within. Each organ has an assigned function. The liver is in charge of planning your life, and its partner, the gallbladder, in decision making.

This means that YOU have the choice to decide how you feel about anything in your life. For example, you can feel bad about something for the rest of your life or choose to change it and no longer use the excuse that it is impossible. Once you become conscious, it is up to you to decide how you emotionally feel or what life patterns you choose.

It is wise to consider your choices and the emotional feelings connected to them to make the correct decision. Because Earth is a place of duality, there are always at least two choices. The choices can have either creative or destructive effects on yourself and others. Even if you are pressured or tricked into making a choice, ultimately, it is you who makes the final decision, and you are the one who will have to live with the consequences.

Both the ego and soul want to participate with you in decision-making. They always communicate with you via emotional language, usually through your third chakra, because this center is the most receptive to all types of emotions. Emotional feelings are just feelings until you give them meaning with words. Therefore, emotions are an original part of the Language of Light, and you can learn to decode what the ego and soul are saying to you.

Ego – The ego primarily communicates via the liver in the physical body.

The ego is connected to the human mind, and the human mind can connect to the Universal Mind. It is an intelligent and masculine energy. The ego is also known as your lower self. It is the essence of physical animal DNA and governs past memories. The ego helps you survive on Earth, as its mission is to protect you by all means. The ego is the record keeper of all your Earth incarnations.

An unbalanced ego will torture you with negative emotions and fear that you gathered during this life or past lives and will try to protect you from repeating anything that caused you emotional trauma, physical harm, or death.

Soul – In the physical body, the soul communicates via the spleen.

The heart chakra is the soul's home. The soul is always connected to Cosmic Love. It is known as your higher self, and it is present in spiritual (cosmic) DNA. The soul is feminine spiritual/emotional energy that governs your future (when not blocked by the ego). The soul is the record keeper of all your cosmic lives.

An unhealed soul worries about the future. It may feel lost, broken, and worried that it will never stop returning to the Earth and will not return back home.

The ego dwells in past memories, and his emotions reflect this. The soul is worried about the future, and her emotions reflect this. Once you recognize their emotional language, you can be centered in your body, in the present, and make your decisions based on true facts instead of the emotional rollercoaster these two can put you on. You can also easily recognize which one needs healing or nurturing.

THREE DOORS OF INFINITE POSSIBILITIES

There are endless possibilities available to all, but sometimes, you fail to recognize them because you cannot see the doors that lead to them. Humans are often blinded by their own personal and collective suffering, and as a result, they might feel limited and stuck.

You are afraid to step into the unknown. You are afraid that you may fail. You are afraid that you are not worthy of this step. You feel you may not be qualified enough, educated enough, or spiritual enough. But the real question is, "When will you be ready to step through the door of infinite possibilities to have a better life? When will you become a reality writer?"

You will be ready to open these new doors once you feel that you are done with suffering, accept all that has happened to you, and surrender to it. The doors of infinite possibilities do not open for those who want only personal gain. They only open when you are willing to serve humanity; naturally, you will also benefit.

First Door – Knowledge

Willingness to change, to embrace love instead of suffering, to stay positive, and to stay optimistic toward any life situation will open the first door to the orange color. Willingness is the key and your doorway into your second chakra. Behind this door, you will observe new ideas, inspiration, creativity, and your abilities. You can figure out what you want to do physically on Earth (you have unlimited choices) while being a beacon of love. You will find that you are safe and supported by your soul (your higher self) and your soul family.

Please know that no one will give you an assignment concerning what to do. If you want to be the creator of your reality, then you need to make that choice. You need to learn to make choices and sound decisions. You need to believe in yourself and what you can offer this world. You are loved, you are worthy, you are intelligent, and you are a being of light occupying a human vessel. What is it that you can offer this world? Dream and imagine.

Meditate with your hands resting over your second chakra. Imagine that your whole body and auric field are filled with orange color. Explore with the enthusiasm and innocence of a little child (that you used to be) what you are good at and what your life mission is. Allow yourself to be guided by your soul.

Second Door - Wisdom

When deciding what your purpose in life is, look at your soul's passion. What is it that you want to be? What can YOU physically create to make this world a better place? When you have an idea, you are ready to open the second door of the green color, the fourth chakra. Honesty and integrity are the keys to this door.

Behind this door, there is no more time to shed your past. That is now a waste of time. You must face your past with compassion, understanding, and positivity toward what happened to you and what brought you here. If you need to forgive or move on, do it quickly. Forgive others and yourself; moving from one place to another requires no more suffering.

You are now ready to work on your plan to manifest your life mission in the physical world. After all, you came to Earth to give a breath of life to dreams of many kinds. Choices will once again arise. What kind of breath will you give to your mission? Will it be of positive intentions, love, honesty, and integrity? Or will you be tempted to take shortcuts? You know there are no shortcuts to divinity or into the field of infinite possibilities. You are at your heart, at the seat of your soul. If you take a shortcut, you will only cheat yourself.

Take physical actions to plan your mission. You are behind the door of freedom. If you can dream and feel it, you are one step closer to manifesting it. The Universe loves bold people. Be free and be bold. Be kind, loving, respectful, and honest with yourself and others. Remember to plan.

Meditate with your hands resting over your fourth chakra. Imagine that your whole body and auric field are filled with green. Explore (with a passion) how to bring your dreams into reality. Allow yourself to be guided by your soul.

Third Door - Soul Memory (Your Devine Ability)

Lastly, the third door is dark blue, representing the sixth chakra. The keys to this door are ultimate trust in God, belief in yourself, and a meaningful (positive) way of life.

Once you walk through this door, you are a divine being dedicating your life to serving all of humanity (via what you chose behind the orange door in the second chakra). Take a leap of faith to fully manifest your life's mission in the 3D world of Earth. Your energy is now in the 5D realm and is supported by the highest available energy. We have your back; we will teach you how to access your Akashic Records, the Christ/Magdalene grid, etc. We support you on your fearless mission to walk through the three doors of infinite possibilities, to be the conscious creator of your own life, to be in charge of your destiny, and to be the reality writer. You are god, and God is you. If you create from the level of unconditional love, without any fears, without any control, and with unwavering trust – you can make a heaven on Earth.

Meditate with your hands resting over the sixth chakra. Imagine that your whole body and auric field are filled with a blue color. Be one with God and allow God to be one with you. Let your intuition guide you, and let the field of infinite possibilities show you how you can be of service with your unique skills. Allow your soul to remind you about your original abilities.

Overview:
First door – Knowledge - Orange color – 2nd Chakra – Key: Willingness – Energy: Dream and Imagine
Second door – Wisdom - Green color – 4th Chakra – Key: Honesty and Integrity – Energy: Doing and Planning
Third door – Soul Power - Dark blue color – 6th Chakra – Key: Trust in God and in Yourself – Energy: Conscious Creator, Reality Writer

Many dreams of this possibility. Only a handful are willing to walk this path in which you sacrifice yourself for others as you find the true essence of your being.

I (inspiration)
A (and)
M (motivation)

CHAPTER 7

FALLING IN LOVE WITH THE HUMAN

You are a divine extraterrestrial being living in a human body. ~ Pleiadians

The secret is out! You are an alien living in a human body, and you have been doing this since the biblical Big Flood. Before the biblical flood, you only experimented with embodying the human vessel while sustaining your entire soul memory. This endeavor had several flaws, as it is not natural for a higher-vibrational soul to incarnate into a lower-vibration physical body. It is logical to assume that the extraterrestrials did not favor embodying the animal vessel, a human body.

The Big Flood is an integral part of history for starseeds as it defines a split between pre-flood and post-flood soul memories. During the pre-flood time, your soul most likely occupied a genetically modified extraterrestrial body, had full soul memory, and had a considerably long-life span. During the post-flood time, your soul could incarnate only into the human body. This featured a primate body that was upgraded with extraterrestrial DNA. This body is pre-programmed to be controlled by fear, is not naturally compatible with higher consciousness, and has a short life span. The short life span made it tricky for humans to realize that they are more than human and have soul rights. To recall your pre-flood extraterrestrial memories, you must accept your past as a fact that you are a human being now, by your free will choice. In other words, you race against time.

FROZEN IN FEAR

The star-seed soul awakening brings a natural curiosity about your existence on other planets. You start looking for answers, which is exciting, but you may also notice an odd feeling that humanity ruined your life or imprisoned you on Earth. Many of you hold this secret resentment inside. However, it will not help you on your spiritual journey in returning home. Resentment has you trapped within the field of resistance (you will learn more about resistance fields in chapter 10). What will help? Fall in love with yourself and humanity rather than rejecting it with the excuse that you long to go home as you no longer want to be imprisoned on Earth.

Earth is a challenging planet to live on. It is a training ground for humans until they become multi-dimensional -planetary beings. As a star-seed, you arrived here a long time ago with the purpose of being a teacher. You accepted the job of guiding humans in their journey. It often feels like you forgot to bring your training manual with you before leaving for this job. It also feels as if you have temporary amnesia concerning your past.

Unfortunately, life in a human body differs significantly from an extraterrestrial body. On your journey through Earth's incarnations, you have experienced both good lifetimes and traumatizing ones. Eventually, fear caused by barbaric human actions, the ferocity of animals, scarcity, and life's difficulties broke you down. All this has been recorded in your DNA and passed down through the generations. Both positive and negative qualities are passed down.

Furthermore, the Sons of Belial created negative energy grids on Earth by reversing some of Earth's powerful Ley lines and vortexes to have mind control. They distorted the human psyche and installed various mind virus programs into susceptible humans (for example, rape, molestation, addiction, killing, violent behavior, theft, etc.). They did this to harvest the emotional energy from the victims and use it to propel their own agenda to gain ultimate control over the human race. The damaging mind programs in humans work similarly to a virus in a computer. The more viruses you have, the faster the infection will spread. The virus instills fear, which then influences the creation of willpower fueled by suffering and negativity. This negatively sourced willpower is what allows the cycles to continue.

Within some past lives, you were forced to take violent actions to protect yourself and others, which is not in your nature (in the original essence of your being). Every lifetime brings about different challenges. When you remember your past lives, do not judge them from the 21st-century point of view. You had to do what you had to do to survive. Life circumstances and values were different in each century. You also might have had lifetimes where you were entirely under the mind control of the Sons of Belial. No wonder the past tends to paralyze you in fear. It sparks questions such as: Could this be true? How could this have happened? Where was my soul family at that time? How could anyone let this happen? As a result, some of you naturally seek to withdraw from humanity, completely losing trust in anyone or anything. You are feeling abandoned and betrayed. You may want to live in seclusion, shelter yourself away from people, or live in a closed spiritual community. There are better solutions than these. Truthfully, you are simply running away from your destiny.

To answer your questions, you have never been alone, and everything that has occurred has a reason. We can only help you after you rise above the feeling of being a victim or a bully. Your job is to learn to be neutral, let go of blaming others for ruining your life, and take responsibility for yourself. You have to do the most challenging part alone because it has to be done by your own free will. You must start the healing process, and we will meet you halfway.

To discover who you are, you first need to accept the human you are, including your past lives and current limitations. Be aware of the fears lurking behind almost every corner; do not let them intimidate you. Instead of being constantly afraid, you must look for knowledge and learn as much as possible about your history. You need to know about positive and negative energy, beings helping you grow, and those who would instead control you. Knowledge is an incredible power that the Sons of Belial robbed you of. You do not need to be afraid when you know what you are facing. You simply need to know how to maneuver through these circumstances. Most of all, do not be scared to fall in love with the human self or with humanity. Would you believe it if we told you this action would free you? Humans may not be perfect, but accepting and surrendering can open many new doors.

GOOD NEWS

Several times throughout your incarnations, you regained your entire soul memory. The Essene time is a perfect tangible example of one of your conscious incarnations and life in the human body. In the Essene time, you were welcomed into the family, which vibrated at the frequency of unconditional love. Love is the essence of your being, and you thrive surrounded by those who love you. You felt safe and protected. You were ready for the mission to unfold slowly over the next 2,000 years.

Your Books of Life are filled with records of your accomplishments, your assistance to humanity, and all of the levels of suffering you have endured within your lifetimes. When you finally connect all of this together in your lifetime, you will get a glimpse of who you are and how powerful you are. At the exact moment, you also face the gruesome reality of how your lives ended. Life has not been easy for those on the Path of Light. You may realize how tired you are. Your ego eagerly shouts out your soul wounds and will want to protect you from any further harm possible caused by the human cruelty in this life. The ego does not know we live in the 21st century or that being eccentric is widely accepted. We know that it is hard to get through all of these memories and that it is hard to figure out how you fit into your human life while trying to recall your ancient extraterrestrial memories.

We hear you that you are tired, that you struggle, and that many of you feel unsupported. We know you might be rejecting the human body, hating your human experience, or possibly wanting to return home. We hear you, but we suggest you consider shifting your thoughts about this into something more positive, as this kind of negative thinking closes more doors than opens.

Planet Earth has been your choice. You have forgotten who you are. Some of you think if you hang out long enough in this body, set your intentions toward leaving, and never again returning, you will magically graduate to the higher planetary system. Your intention itself is not good enough. You have to become a doer, a conscious participant in healing both the human and the alien parts of you. This also means loving and accepting both sides of you. Only those who are in acceptance, love, and peace with everything that has happened on Earth are allowed to live among existing higher dimensional multi-planetary beings without space for bickering, hate, revenge, or nonsense wars.

The body is a gift, and your human incarnation is a gift to all of us. You have the ultimate power to make changes in your world. All the changes you make create a ripple effect that impacts all of us. As you heal your human self, you simultaneously heal the alien self and your soul family.

Let us metaphorically look into the dynamics of your vessel.

Your body is like a computer. When you were born, your soul and ego brought their own software. The software they brought is not compatible with each other. They alternate their programs every seven years to reach some compromise (as they have to share this body). For seven years, you go through feelings of being safe physically and financially over feeling creative and spiritual. In the following seven years, the favored feeling will flip and become vice versa.

Once in a while, the ego and soul may try to corrupt each other's software. This can cause great havoc, conflict, and even computer malfunction (your body). Unfortunately, the ego and soul forgot they had the knowledge to upgrade the computer. They could work on their own software versions to make them compatible. They just need to work together as a team.

This is currently happening for many of you. You are forcing the 5D advanced spiritual software to run on an outdated 3D computer. Your ego is hogging a considerable amount of space in your memory bank to run its own program in the background. You keep your fingers crossed, hoping the ego does not accidentally download harmful malware into the computer.

In your life on Earth, you can make your 3D body compatible with 5D energy. The secret lies within your nervous system. The Essenes did it, and so can you. It is encoded within your DNA. Your ego and soul know how to refurbish your computer so that you can accomplish all of this. The first step is to fall back in love with the human that you are. You are a divine being living in a human vessel. It may not be perfect, but it has many hidden abilities that you are completely ignoring. You need to fall back in love with your human self to serve humanity. Secondly, fill your life with humor. Humor is a great healer. There is no need to be serious all the time. Discipline is the key to success, but humor lightens the heart and fills the soul with joy.

ACCEPTING YOURSELF EXERCISE:

1. Look in a mirror. Look deeply into your eyes.

2. Say aloud or in your mind, "I am a divine being living in this human body." (If you know where you came from, you can say I am a Pleiadian living in this human body). Say it as a factual statement.

3. "I love myself and my human vessel. I accept this life and claim this vessel as the vehicle for my divine higher self."

4. "I LOVE YOU, and I love my soul family, who I know is listening to me right now."

5. "I can do this life. I am in service to humanity."

You can then continue this conversation with yourself or go on about your day.

CHAPTER 8

ACCEPTING THE ALIEN

*Giving knowledge is a form of love. Sharing
knowledge with humanity is sharing love with humanity.
~ Pleiadians*

After the destruction of Atlantis, the communication
and transportation between planetary systems were
temporarily disabled. No one knew how extensive the
damage was outside the Earth. A few days without
sophisticated technology awakened severe questions.
What happened to our connection and communication
with other planetary systems and beings? What
happened to our solar satellites? Why did no AI
technology correct the issues? What happened to our
central transportation center located on Mars? Did our
family and loved ones stationed close to Earth and Mars
survive? How long would it take until we see them
again? The technological disconnection was rather
shocking to all of us. The repairs that we believed could
have been fixed within a few days ended up spanning a
few hundred years.

Soon, it dawned on us that answers would be
lacking. Reality eventually hit. We were stuck on Earth
and forced to work with the only resources, technology,

and medicine we had. We quickly had to become self-sustainable to survive. As if that was not enough, fights among some extraterrestrials left on the Earth had erupted over the remaining resources. The lives of extraterrestrials changed from being free-spirited researchers to becoming survivalists. This was a significant step back for all extraterrestrial beings, regardless of whether they were on the Path of Light or on the Path of Dark.

Many suffered from the emotions of a broken heart. There were many star beings whose family members were visiting other planets at the time of the disaster. At the time, star beings were also traveling to other planetary systems, such as the Pleiades, to obtain certain medicines that would heal them (or others) from the physical ailments encountered on Earth. We could not make several medicines we needed on Earth, as we lacked the plants to make them. Moreover, without the necessary medicine to heal these ailments, they soon proved to be fatal. We experienced a traumatic decrease in our population as well as the loss of communication with our families on other planets. To further assist you in imagining this, this could be compared to a situation where there is suddenly no transportation or communication between your continents. Depending on where you live, you must rely only on what you can utilize. We truly experienced despair and hopelessness for the first time.

Before the destruction, many refused to accept that the Children of the Law of One had raised awareness about this situation. For the last 6,000 years, they spoke of a tangible link between achieving a major goal and total destruction if the balance between feminine and masculine energy was not kept.

Generally, when the goal (for example, Atlantis) is achieved with the force of power, lacking a solid foundation of knowledge and wisdom (being in harmony with Earth and the Universe), the eventual natural outcome is destruction. Atlantis did not resonate with the will of God (it was not in a cosmic resonance flow), so it did not last. It did have the potential to be successful, but eventually, the masculine energy overpowered everything else (more about this principle in the tenth chapter).

NEW LIFE IN EGYPT

After the destruction of Atlantis, we moved and adjusted to a new life in Egypt. Since that time, you have known us as ancient Egyptians. Our primary focus became to (once again) cultivate and maintain our natural 5D spiritual abilities to sustain our physical bodies and our ability to hold high frequencies in both mind and body. In Atlantis's golden days, many beings did not care for this and let their abilities slowly diminish. We were stellar in our abilities during the time of Lemuria, but time changes everything. Believe it or not, the Atlantean technology spoiled us. This is what is happening to you today. (As we have before, we point out that technology is not bad as long as it does not control you.) The wise teachers and healers among us became the most important beings who assisted us in moving forward. They taught us to be patient, to stay in our hearts, and to stay connected to the Source while we waited for the planetary transportation and communication system to be restored.

Even though our lives had changed dramatically, we were grateful that we survived. We connected with other extraterrestrial tribes already living on various parts of Earth. Later, we accepted that the Annunaki upgraded primates with our extraterrestrial DNA (which they stole from the Surrogate Crystal God) to create the human race.

Ancient Egypt was a cradle for those on the Path of Light. We required everyone who desired to join our way of life to follow strict rules of discipline. We hoped these rules would ensure the purity of the soul and the ultimate survival of the Children of the Law of One. This was successful, as you are here today, reading these words and rekindling ancient memories. We love you, Child of the Law of One.

We had hoped that our tragedy would have brought everyone closer together. Those on the Path of Light merged more with humans and began to bestow our ancient knowledge upon them. Giving knowledge is a form of love. Sharing our knowledge with humanity was sharing our love with humanity.

We began to teach humans how to grow food, make safe shelters, live honorable lives, and to avoid wars at all cost. When one has knowledge, one does not need to suffer in fear, be hungry, sick, cold, or abused. We treated them equally and hoped that they would be like us. After all, they were our children. We prayed that they would understand that mastering the Path of Light takes time and determination. Over time, Egyptian Mystery Schools became a popular place for humans to cultivate their abilities and spend some time in the presence of what they called gods. To our disappointment, not everyone strived for self-mastery. Many just wanted instant power to be like us without proper learning.

Those who sought instant power chose to follow the Path of Dark. The Sons of Belial, who were also thriving on Earth, were quietly running their agenda to take over the world by manipulating humans to do their bidding. They lured the humans in with glamorous and deceiving shortcuts. They offered power that was granted within a short period of time. This kind of power never lasts.

Beings on the Path of Dark came from the same Source as those on the Path of Light. Ultimately, we all have the same parents. We just make different choices. The leaders of the Sons of Belial built their foundation based on the same principles as the Children of the Law of One. This foundation is knowledge and wisdom. The Sons of Belial granted their followers temporary power, rapid growth, and power over cities and countries.

However, the Sons of Belial refused to give their followers access to knowledge on maintaining their power. Therefore, to have power as a follower of the Sons of Belial, you must be in constant contact with them. So long as you use their power, they control you. They inflict fear upon their followers to further control them. They want their followers to believe that they are nothing without them, that they are nothing without their borrowed and limited power. Naturally, this fear allows easy manipulation. The Sons of Belial keep this knowledge from them to keep their followers trapped.

There is a straightforward difference between the Dark and Light. Receive what we share with you in neutral emotions (without judgment).

The Path of Dark offers shortcuts. It will dangle promises of abundance and rapid rise to power (money, status, influence, recovery from illness, abilities, etc). However, its effect is temporary and will fade since you will manifest harmful abundance. This will cause you to suffer through emotional and physical pain. The Path of Dark is manipulative. It knows that you will blame God for giving up on you rather than blaming them. This creates further disconnection from the original Source while being trapped in the Game of Life.

The Path of Light takes considerably longer. There are no shortcuts to enlightenment; there is constant learning and practice. When one surrenders to the will of God, this path could be filled with happiness and unconditional love, but it is a constant moment of striving to lead an honorable life and be in service. It leads you into your true soul memory and ultimate positive abundance. It also leads you toward the exit within this Game of Life.

FROM MAJORITY TO MINORITY

In ancient Egypt, you could still freely express who you were and what you could do because it was typical back then. You had no need to hide the true essence of your being, as you subconsciously do today, to protect yourself from harm. You were not afraid of other aliens or humans. After all, extraterrestrials were still the majority of the living beings. Everyone knew you were different. Being different was normal and more than welcome. However, as time went on, everything changed.

Humanity was growing at an accelerated rate. We could not help but secretly wonder when the Council of Light would find out that the Annunaki created the new species they called human beings. We also worried because some extraterrestrials had fallen in love with human beings and created families with them. What would the Council of Light say about that? Their babies were growing up, inheriting considerable abilities that ordinary humans lacked. Some were eager to learn and keep on the Path of Light, while others just looked for shortcuts, were seduced by false promises, and showed off their ego before their kindness of the soul. Sadly, many regular humans followed this pattern.

Despite our extended life span, we are not immortal. Since rejuvenating medicines from the other planets were no longer available, our bodies began to age and suffer from diseases. We scrambled to utilize the herbal remedies we could make from the plants we had before the destruction. Slowly, as time went on, the number of extraterrestrials decreased. Our communities became much smaller as we had no considerable desire to repopulate ourselves in numbers as the humans did. Eventually, we became the minority.

We did our best to assist our souls in being reborn in our godly bodies. Alternatively, we guided our souls (in the afterlife) to a place where they could wait until a body became available. Since we anchored our soul's DNA in the Earth realm (when we accepted animal DNA to upgrade our body), our soul (after death) did not soar up high enough to connect with our soul group. Part of it remained in the realm of Earth (known as your shadow or ego). We were concerned about this and did not wish for any soul to be lost. Since we learned to track our soul after it left its bodily vehicle, we created several places to host these souls. The inner Earth assisted us in this challenging task. We left Egyptian scrolls and books containing knowledge regarding this. The soul is a conscious energy and could be compared to a precious memory chip. We did not want our souls to get lost in-between dimensions. We also did not want our souls getting into the hands of the wrong people.

KEEPING BALANCE

As time went on, the Sons of Belial started to spread false rumors that those who killed a god would be able to harness that god's entire essence. This became quite a Dark Age for all extraterrestrials. First, we became the minority. Next, we had to start hiding our presence. We cloaked our glowing auras so we appeared like humans. We had an opportunity to retreat into the inner Earth but wanted to be in service. A few of us left and were happy for them, but many of us stayed to live on the surface of the Earth to keep the balance between the Dark and Light energies.

Gods, Enlightened Ones, Magis, or any other names you know them by were beings within your soul family. They knew how to work with the elements and could command spirits (demonic and angelic). For example, King Solomon could. They knew how to direct prana to connect with the soul for the effect of bodily healing like Jesus could, and they could energize objects with magical powers like Merlin could, to name a few examples from history. Many held, as you would call it, supernatural abilities and power. Some humans desired to have this without taking the time to gain the knowledge necessary to master it, so these enlightened beings (YOU) became the endangered species of the realm of Earth.

Some humans thought they could steal the energy of the gods by forcing them to pass their essence to them. Of course, this is impossible; the essence of one soul would not willingly walk into another person's body, especially when the intent of holding this energy was hostile. Humans often held these gods hostage until they decided to kill them and supposedly gain their essence by eating the god's heart or by drinking their blood. They were misled by a false belief given to them by those on the Path of Dark. These gods could have easily killed the humans and escaped, but they would rather sacrifice themself than harm another.

The mistake we made was not claiming our BOUNDARIES. We treated everyone equally and believed they would return the same act of kindness. Our heart was naturally giving. Saying NO and claiming our boundaries was not in our nature; eventually, we burned out. Another mistake we recognized was that we acted like overprotective parents and made decisions for everyone, not on our consciousness level, instead of allowing them to make their own choices (good or bad). We did not ask if humans wanted our assistance; we assumed that everyone wanted to be healed and grow (like us), so we dived into saving humanity. We volunteered to save everyone, but to our dismay, only some were willing to be saved. Perhaps it was just us who really needed soul healing at that time because we felt we failed.

While God's energy belongs to everyone, one must find their own way to connect with this energy. One can do this by finding worthiness through honorable life actions. One's soul can be purified by learning from past mistakes in one's life. Through this process, one can quickly be reconnected with God's consciousness frequency. Good things come to those who practice positivity. One cannot be greedy, harm others, or surround himself with negativity and expect to have the birthright to all knowledge.

All energy follows the same basic set of laws. You receive what you are. What you give will come back to you threefold. For example, if you wish negativity on others, this energy will return to you, triple what you put out. The same goes for positivity. These energy laws apply to absolutely everyone in this Universe, without exception. When negativity started returning to humans and impacting them, they blamed everyone else instead of taking responsibility for their actions.

We reconnected back with the Source and started to balance Cosmic Resistance through positivity and unconditional love. You are continuing in this work today. You are helping to assure that Earth (along with humanity) will have an inspiring future. Reminders of who you are still exist in Egypt and worldwide today in buildings, statutes, drawings, and more. Most of these forms are visible as your eyes are the windows to your soul. Your soul is meant to assist you in remembering who you are.

Preserving the knowledge of our teaching material to pass it down to future generations (in case you still need it) became one of our top priorities. The ancient version of these teachings is still around today and was crafted through conscious layers of energy. By accessing these ancient teachings, you gain knowledge. By practicing it, you gain wisdom. This wisdom will connect you with your higher self, who can guide you in rediscovering your ancient soul memory. This will allow you to cultivate the abilities you once had and attract positive abundance.

These soul teachings were documented on various tablets during the early times (starting in Atlantis) and later rewritten into books (in several languages). These teachings became secret and were quietly passed down from generation to generation in oral, written, and visual (art) forms. Ancient teachings purposely bypass fast growth into power, which is almost always self-destructive. Before you become the master, you have to be the successful apprentice.

YOU ARE NOT A FAILURE

Remembering your ancient history allows you to forgive and accept your true self. After you master overcoming lower human energies, you can access your ancient extraterrestrial knowledge and your soul memory. These are sources of your hidden power.

Many of you store an odd and unexplained inner feeling of failure and unworthiness in your spiritual DNA. You feel stuck in your life and are afraid of moving forward to pursue your dreams. Sometimes, you feel that you should just hide, especially if you are pursuing spiritual study or spiritual-based work.

You may have a good reputation, be respected by your peers and family, have a solid education, and a good job, yet you may secretly feel that you are disappointing those around you. In your mind, you believe that you have somehow faked your way into accomplishing your achievements. In reality, you logically understand that you have not faked anything and have worked hard to be where you are today. Still, you secretly continue to feel like a failure and fake anyway. Therefore, you try to hide these feelings from those around you because you fear they would not want to be your friend (coworker, client, business partner, etc) if they figure out you are fake and unworthy. These feelings are exhausting.

If you experience this (not everyone does), you have activated your past lives' low vibrational memories, but instead of looking into them, you locked them away because you are afraid of what you will find. This action also prevents good memories from resurfacing from the same period. Your current 21st-century ego-based mind translates these vague past lives memories into full-blown shame so everyone can see it (it is its odd way to protect you) instead of showing you the truth and good memories and chance to lose control over you.

Feeling shame is just an energetically imprinted memory with the message, "Look at me; I have failed (in something)." Therefore, when you start feeling this ancient shame, you can get excited because there is no lower energy than that, and you can finally ask, "What is it that I failed at?" It truly is not as bad as it feels.

The truth is that we all have failed at one point or another. We failed when we set foot in Lemuria because it led to where we are today. But how can we accept that everything was a failure? We all collectively grew from the Earth experience and must accept that everything happens for a reason. Failure is just an opportunity for learning and transformation. In the world of duality, failure is the best teacher.

Should you hide because you were a highly evolved extraterrestrial being who made a mistake in the Earth realm? Maybe you made a wrong choice, but no one is left to judge that except yourself. Perhaps the circumstances forced you to make decisions you would typically not make. How many times have humans been compelled to become survivors? The same happened to you.

In the pre-flood period, you were intelligent and conscious beings trying to do your best. But later on, you feared that your best was not good enough because it was based on the fight for survival.

These feelings of shame, guilt, fear, failure, anxiety, etc., should only remind you of who you are. Shame and guilt are not something one should dwell on forever. Forgiveness to yourself and others will heal the failure, and acceptance of your worthiness will replace the shame. Then, unconditional love will open a door toward a higher consciousness where failure is no longer a concern.

- Set your boundaries. It is acceptable to say no when pressured or obligated to do something.

- Respect other people's choices. The unconditional love approach is to respect one's choice and let the consequences (good or bad) teach life lessons. Be the parent who waits patiently until the child asks for a helping hand.

Offer your assistance to those who want it. The right people will find you once you put out what you are offering. Learn to distinguish between those who genuinely want to be helped and those who just want to take advantage of you. Remember your boundaries.

CHAPTER 9

CLOSING YOUR EXTRATERRESTRIAL CONSCIOUSNESS

The extraterrestrial soul memories are a priceless treasure. ~ Pleiadians

Communication lines between Earth and other planets were eventually repaired, and star beings built a new stargate station that allowed them to fly to and from Earth. Following that, the Council of Light discovered the fast-growing human race and our collective involvement in their life. You already know that we have pleaded for the survival of the human race. The Council of Light was willing to listen to our reasoning and, after considerable deliberation, offered us a deal. The deal was that they would give humanity a chance to evolve with the stipulation that the humans would be closely monitored and periodically assessed to determine whether they were on the path to becoming benevolent beings or on a path to self-destruction.

We felt that we had to become their teachers to assist humanity in the evolution that the Council of

Light was looking for; therefore, we volunteered to be teachers. There was a catch. To be able to teach humans, we had to agree to be incarnated into human bodies. The Council of Light had created the rule that after the biblical Big Flood, the gods (extraterrestrials) could no longer walk in extraterrestrial bodies among humans. Those who intended to assist from the higher dimension could only do so as invisible guides and would be allowed to only give limited guidance to those who would listen. We also had to follow the rule that no being of light, without having a physical body, could participate in any material creation on Earth. This is why most of us prefer to incarnate into the body as it provides us an opportunity to create something solid, such as a book, medical cure, invention, etc., that can last longer than the human body of one incarnation and could also help make the Earth a better place.

Another rule we agreed to was that once incarnated into the human body, we would not remember our divine soul's memories as it was unsafe for our mission. This chapter will explain this later under "Our soul memory."

We accepted these conditions because we love humanity and took this as an opportunity to teach by example. Many of us walk among you, and many reading our books are us. We knew that once we entered the human incarnation, we would need a little help on our journey as there were many life situations we could not control. Therefore, we prepared several triggering situations that remind us that we are not ordinary humans and have a higher calling.

1. Our ancient memory of who we are

Everyone has to cross the River of Forgetfulness and experience memory amnesia before taking on a human body.

To help us remember, we set up a series of painful triggers to awaken our memories with shock. The nervous system of the body is like a psychic antenna. If triggered with a shock, the antenna becomes temporarily more receptive. Receiving some information from the higher self is intended to push one to embark on a journey searching for more ancient knowledge. The exception to avoid this trigger applies when you are born in an already established family of light where family members lovingly assist you in awakening your sleeping memory to avoid painful triggers.

2. Our human family

There is no guarantee into which family we would incarnate our soul (this still applies today), even though we tried to control this as much as possible.

To help us, we secretly arranged for a few to incarnate without crossing the River of Forgetfulness so they could establish communities of soul families. These individuals were trained in Light and/or conscious conception (which were later passed on to the Essenes). These conceptions assisted in bringing the selected souls who desired to serve humanity into fully awakened families who would support them from birth and help them with knowledge and initiations. Some also mastered cellular rejuvenation and became temporary immortals, extending their lifetime in the human body. This was because they could have enough time to share the ancient wisdom teachings with others, keep records of oral and written form, and successfully pass these teachings to future generations.

3. Our soul's memory

Why must we sacrifice our soul's memory with all its vast ancient knowledge? Until the human incarnation, our soul memory was fully embodied in our extraterrestrial genetically modified bodies. True knowledge holds great power (always remember that power has two facets – positive and negative).

Since we could hold significant amounts of electromagnetic energy within the body, we appeared to have supernatural abilities and shining bodies. For example, those who cultivated their abilities could easily tune themselves to hold the frequency of various dimensions within their 3D bodies. This allowed us to move on the astral plane, communicate between dimensions, and be consciously connected to the Universal Mind and Cosmic Love. It was a difficult decision to give this up, but carrying our soul memory when incarnated into an earth family would be unrealistic and extremely dangerous for those enlightened beings entering the human body as they would be easier to recognize and become targets for the Sons of Belial.

The other reason to separate our soul's memory was that the physical human body is not naturally compatible with holding 5D and higher energies in which soul memories are stored. The human body needs adjustments before downloading its full soul consciousness (memory) into the nervous system; otherwise, the body's physical health could be compromised.

We also had to learn to work with the human ego, part of the human being. The untamed ego looks for any shortcuts that will allow it to access the soul's memories without first ensuring that the mind, body, and soul are appropriately trained to receive the information. Misunderstood soul memories in the human body could be dangerous and do more harm than good. It should also be noted that soul memories used for rapid advancement or manipulation will eventually turn against you. It is the same as matches in the wrong hands starting a forest fire.

We supported the Council of Light in the decision to seal our soul memory (hiding our abilities) for our protection until we could find a way to remember (preferably through spiritual growth) who we are and regain trust in the one True God (oneness) while overcoming the deception of imposters. This applied to every extraterrestrial being, whether on The Path of Light or the Path of Dark.

We were not afraid of this decision because we knew that starting with ancient Atlantis when we were known as the Children of the Law of One, we had begun creating a wealthy depository, full of divine knowledge and records, that would stay hidden on Earth so we could access it as needed. Records written on tablets (and later in books) are hidden in the inner cities of Earth. Ancient coded knowledge was deposited into plants and minerals. Since knowledge is a form of energy, we also weaved it into art, buildings, and ancient sites so it would be in plain sight on the surface of Earth and freely available to any soul willing to acknowledge it. We created energy time capsules with various downloads to be available to anyone with the correct spiritual frequency code and also left encoded messages in our spiritual DNA. This is where our strength is. We are the bringers of knowledge, and we believed back then that, given the proper tools, we - you (in the future) would be capable of retracing our ancient memories.

We had given the Council of Light a protocol to close our hearts (the seat of the soul) and suppress our soul's memory. We created a protective seal (you may know it as an implant or seal) that would separate the soul's divine memory from the human heart at the time of incarnation or birth, as you may call it. From then on, the soul's divine memory is hidden like a priceless ancient artifact outside the body. When one reaches a certain level of soul growth, his higher self will guide him in removing the seal and downloading its extraterrestrial consciousness (soul memory). This was meant to prevent misuse of power by those on the Path of Light and those on the Path of Dark. Believe it or not, we all follow the same protocol.

CLOSING THE HEART

Closing our hearts was a difficult decision but necessary for the survival of the Family of Light. The heart is the seat of the soul. It is the central sun of your being, the solar disk that holds the soul's memory and, therefore, a gateway to all your extraterrestrial abilities. Closing the heart means we have outsourced our soul memory to a different place. We call this place a Soul Cave.

Though we've sealed and closed off the heart, we intentionally left one energy strand in the heart open, which is the connection to Cosmic Love. You are always connected to Cosmic Love through the beating of the heart. Your soul family can communicate with you through Cosmic Love in the language of emotions, the language of your infinite soul. Therefore, we could all experience the love of our soul, family, and God. We had hoped that the language of love would guide us in finding the knowledge needed to remove the seal and open the whole heart.

Emotions are part of the Language of Light, which we encourage you to learn to decipher. The cognitive understanding of how we created this seal has been blocked off by disconnecting part of the energy nervous system pathway between the heart and mind. The seal is sitting in the pineal gland and is programmed with resistant energy (more in chapter ten). This was designed to discourage the unworthy ones from finding a way to remove it. Metaphorically, it is like the hammer the god Thor possesses; only a worthy one can lift it.

THE ESSENES KNEW HOW TO OPEN THE SEAL

The sacred knowledge of how to open the seal and access your soul memory to activate the seat of your soul, your heart (your solar disk), has discretely been passed down from soul family to soul family all around the world since ancient times. For example, the Pharaoh Akhenaten's family passed the knowledge down to their descendants, who later became known as the Essenes. The ancients thoughtfully preserved this knowledge for you in words and drawings inscribed into stone so that one day, when you find them, your soul will remember. Have you noticed the ancient art from Egypt depicting solar disks hovering in the sky and emitting rays of energy onto specific individuals? These ancient engravings and paintings are left behind so that you can understand how the extraterrestrial consciousness (memory) is downloaded into your human consciousness once you are ready to receive it. The solar disk hovering above the individual represents the Soul Cave, and the rays coming out of the solar disk represent the soul memory.

We often refer to the Essenes because they existed during the period of Jesus Christ approximately 2000 years ago. A period that most of you can relate to because of modern-day religious beliefs and teachings about Jesus Christ and the people that lived during that time. This enables your mind to connect more easily with that timeline, especially when you step into the energy fields or find the ancient clues that they left hidden within the Earth for you to find. Many Essenes were beings of light living in human bodies, the same as you are today. Long before that period, they were known as the Egyptian gods, goddesses, and other deities. Some lived in different parts of the world and went by other names but were still considered gods and goddesses by the people of that period. Before that, they were Atlanteans, and some were Lemurians. This is your ancestry lineage. Please note that the last time you fully embodied your soul memory was most likely during your lifetime with the Essenes.

SOUL FAMILY HEALING

The life of star beings in the human body has been challenging, especially for the last 2,000 years. Let us focus on this particular timeframe as it holds the most soul damage and is still relatively recent. You need significant soul healing from this period before you can reenter your ancient alien soul memory. As mentioned, your memory does not reside within your human body but has been outsourced into your Soul Cave. Only your higher self knows how to access and bring this energy back.

Many of you had been called to join the Essenes community, incarnating in their families and continuing to hold the spiritual DNA blueprint until today. You kept incarnating until the planned collective incarnation of now in the 21st century, especially during the crossing of the old and new calendars in 2012 when the Mayan calendar ended, along with its predictions. After 2012, we entered a rare period that may last until 2033. A period of time where you can be the reality writers that can alter the course of Earth for the better. Please note that we/you are not the only ones aware of this knowledge. The dark side is also aware, and they have the same opportunity to be reality writers and alter the course of the Earth to what fits their own agenda.

Therefore, we wish for you to understand the life of the Essenes, where you were taught how to embody your soul memory while in the human body. Before the death and resurrection of Christ, your Essenes families lived closer together, and it was safe to stay in contact with one another. The divine gatherings, energy initiations, and meditations (even when held in distant places) were perfectly planned so everyone could attend. Your soul was dancing with gratitude, joy, and happiness from these events and opportunities, allowing you to stay in close physical contact with those you fully loved and trusted. Then, approximately after 50AD, core family members decided it was safer to hide to survive persecution. Gradually, it became unsafe to freely use your abilities outside your trusted family because the Romans and others would find you and kill you. Families worked together and cleverly relocated Children of Light worldwide (especially in northern and eastern Europe) to carry on the divine work in secrecy. Since that time, you visited your extended soul family only once every few years. You missed them so much. This caused you to start questioning this mission. Your divine soul understood, but your human part suffered from separation. Those were difficult days, yet you persevered and held on to unconditional love, which became the light in the days of darkness.

Around 1,000 AD, people were openly jealous, greedy, and envious of your abilities. Many did not want to understand that they could cultivate their energy and skills and reach your level because that would take years of discipline, which they were unwilling to invest. Instead, it was easier for them to get close to you and take advantage of your kindness. If you did not do what they wanted, they would despise you, and approximately by 1,200 AD, they called you a witch. Only a few treated you as an equal without demanding something from you. As time and incarnations went on, you became more tired and frustrated. As the knowledge brought forth by Jesus Christ and Mary Magdalene slowly dwindled, the truly devoted became fewer and fewer. During a horrific era of witch hunts, you began to silently question, "Is this a blessing or a curse?"

Life in the human body was much more complex than ever imagined. Some of you were experiencing sickness, living in a body with malfunctions, and were shocked to see how humans treated one another. When they worshipped or feared someone, they treated this person well but were often cruel to each other. "Are we failing to teach them?" you wondered.

There were times when you experienced floods of anger and frustration with humanity. You loved them unconditionally, but you experienced firsthand the greed, nonsense, and absurdity outside your communities. Many people thrived because the Sons of Belial showed them shortcuts to gain immediate glory. The Sons of Belial used this to have control over them. At times, this made you feel hopeless. You were grateful that you had each other and your soul families. Life in the human body is hard, but no one can blame others for our choices.

More and more people stopped caring about cultivating their abilities, working toward spiritual immortality, being one with the Universe, and staying on the Path of Light. As centuries passed, the Essenes changed their name over and over to protect the Children of Light. During those years, you took on different genders and roles. Perhaps you have even been one of the very few known as physical immortals. Immortals were hidden among the Family of Light and were the most protected secret. To guard this secret or to protect an immortal was an automatic death sentence for you, your family, and your whole community if the wrong person found out!

Who were the immortals? Upon their readiness and spiritual dedication, several members of the Essenes community were introduced to the arduous initiation of the Rites of Sepulchre that would allow them to prolong the life span of their physical bodies. The only reason for remaining within a human body past the average life span was to serve humanity. In their case, they became the record keepers, or you could call them living librarians. Living librarians have been initiating one another since the fall of Atlantis. You cannot choose to be one. You must be selected. These brave people would dedicate their entire lives to rewriting ancient scriptures and physically keeping ancient wisdom alive to be secretly passed down to future generations. They would teach as well. Some of the teachings were so sacred that they would be passed from one to another only by word of mouth and only when the student reached the level of consciousness to grasp the meaning of the teaching. Once again, the Essenes received knowledge from the Ancient Egyptians, and the Ancient Egyptians received it from Atlantis. The Children of the Law of One secretly thrived using many different names throughout history, not allowing outsiders to make the connection to their ancestors. Outsiders would speculate but could not find the proof to expose them.

We created energy links connecting all of us so that we would recognize each other. These links were meant to trigger your memories. This is why you feel irresistibly drawn to one another when you meet someone who shared a life with you in the past, especially in the Essenes times. The reason is that you automatically exchange light codes, and you both may need soul healing, which you can offer one another. Just to be in each other's presence could be very healing. However, do not confuse this sacred connection with romantic love unless all the past has been healed and you still share the same romantic feelings for each other.

Before you allow the intimate romantic feeling to cloud your mind when you meet someone with whom you have shared countless lifetimes and spiritual journeys, investigate your past-life connections. Learn to distinguish between feelings of unconditional love without any wants or needs and conditional love with many terms and restrictions.

Someone you have shared initiations with, protected the most significant secrets with, and assisted while your soul was journeying in other worlds could be someone who returned into your life for soul healing (yours or theirs), but perhaps not as your life partner. It could be someone you are connected with on the soul level for eternity because he/she is part of your soul family. There is nothing more intimate than a pure soul connection in unconditional love. This kind of love brings knowing into your bodily senses instead of arousal that many imagine while thinking of an intimate soul connection. Meeting soul family members that walk in Earthly bodies, as you do, is a blessing that makes this journey more enjoyable. Hold each of them in a warm embrace of unconditional love, and empower them with wishes of tremendous success. Just as a parent wishes their children to do better than they have, holding a wish or a vision for someone else to succeed in something that may surpass you is sharing unconditional love.

Soul healing brings strength to the heart, peace to the mind, and confidence to the body. What you share will be returned to you threefold.

CHAPTER 10

FIELDS OF RESISTANCE

Understanding, mastering, and passing the fields of resistance were taught in Mystery schools. Today, the Mystery school curriculum is perfectly woven into everyday life. ~ Pleiadians

Resistance is just an energy field you must pass through to open your heart and claim your soul memory. The first two resistance fields are just a collection of false beliefs you were conditioned to accept as true beliefs. These beliefs manifest in real life as strands of chaotic events that create a false reality (yes, absolutely real), blocking you from achieving your goal of healing the fragmented self and manifesting your soul's mission.

This could be different for each individual. The strength of your current resistance field is based on the level of your soul's self-worthiness but not the ego's self-worthiness. The lower your self-worth, the stronger your resistance. Each resistance field allows you to look deeper into your life lessons and decide whether you learned from them. If you did:

- Are you done with suffering?
- Can you surrender and let go?
- Can you let your higher self-guide you?
- Are you willing to embody unconditional love as your creative willpower to realize that you are worthy to claim your original energies back and that you will know how to use them to be in service?

There are three levels of resistance.

PERSONAL RESISTANCE

I am not worthy.

This belief is deeply hidden in your fourth chakra within your soul, echoing with words like, "I am not good enough, I am not worthy of love. I am a failure, I struggle, I am poor, I am sick, etc."

Positive affirmation: *I accept myself. I am worthy. I love my whole self (physical and spiritual) unconditionally.*

Once you begin consciously recognizing your resistance, you can replace that negative voice within you with positive affirmations, and your daily personal resistance will decrease noticeably. Be aware that you are altering your unique personal pattern deeply rooted in your psyche. It has been part of you for a long time and is controlled by your ego. Your ego will let you have this step, but it will almost always try to re-root your old self while in your dream state, especially in your lucid dreaming state.

In lucid dreaming, you become conscious in your dream and experience life situations or parallel realities influenced by your fearful ego. This will feel as real as your awakened state, and you often fully remember the details. You may experience dreams of shame (being naked in public places), dreams of failure where you are not able to accomplish your goal no matter how hard you try, dreams of forgetfulness where you forget to make an essential meal for the family, forget to pick up kids from school, or forget to go to work, etc. These dreams want to instill in your thoughts that you are a failure, no one loves you, and there is no good reason to try to change your life.

When you wake up from a nightmare like this, just take a few deep breaths and remind yourself to stay in the present moment. Put your left hand on your belly and your right hand on your forehead and focus on your breathing or the "Ohm" sound. This will help you bring you back into the present. If you still experience unsettles, you may also try the Pranayama cooling breath technique, where you roll your tongue and take a few breaths in and out through the roll of your tongue to cool down your Vagus nerve.

Set boundaries and keep a to-do list for the day. Center your full, conscious attention only on this day, staying positive and moving forward. Sometimes, you just need to take it easy, only one day at a time.

Once you become fully aware of your lucid dreaming (to some people, this also happens while astral projecting), you can consciously become the boss of this energy and turn the ego's torture into healing and empowerment. Your dream state energy is profound, manifesting energy from which your ego does not want you to gain knowledge. With some practice, you can master this energy and use it consciously to manifest anything you want during that dream. In lucid dreams, the astral plane, parallel realities, or meditations, your physical body is safely resting where you left it while your energy body travels. In other words, you are a being made of energy, not a solid mass. You have a hundred percent free will in this energy form, making manifesting anything you want in that particular place easier. You are like a god there.

Are you naked in a public place? Give yourself clothes and tell yourself there is no need to feel ashamed. Did your business fail? Then think, how can you help to save it? It does not have to be realistic as in everyday life, but it must be positive. For example, if you do not have enough money to keep the business going, you can make yourself win the lottery or find a treasure in your attic. Be creative with your imagination. If you can imagine it while in your dream, it will happen in that dream. Then the result could be like this, you opened your business, and it is successful, you are in service to many people, and life is good. When you wake up, you will be filled with a sense of accomplishment and empowerment, like I got this. If the part of you in the realms of energy is happy and thriving, you should automatically be, too. You know that to be successful, for example, means to be creative. When one thing is not working, then the other will. The realm of energy will provide you with many positive inspirations and possibilities if you are willing to listen. Remember, every action has a reaction.

While dealing with the personal resistance field, be aware of your weaknesses. The ego is the most significant contributor here. Still, you will also encounter negative energy that will try to stop you because it thrives from the resistance level filled with the energy of suffering and fear. It is like an all-you-can-eat buffet. Once you pass this level, THEY have one less soul contributing to it, and of course, it worries "them" that you will teach others how to do it.

Do not make a big fuss about this negative energy. It is just energy. This energy sees your weaknesses and will supply you with false positive good energy to keep you trapped in the realm of illusion. For example, if you desire to be in love with a cosmic being, you may suddenly meet a dreamy, energetic being (in your mind). You may fall in love and enjoy this connection for the rest of your life. In your mind, it will be as accurate as you wish. Physically, it may feel real as well. Still, this being will never be an actual physical person who can take you on a romantic dinner at your favorite restaurant, and you will soon start disconnecting from reality and living a false fantasy. Benevolent beings of light would not mislead you like this.

Do you want to be a superhero and save the world? This same negative energy will guide you to other dimensions, give you weapons of your choice, and convince you that you are saving the Earth while battling evil villains. It will convince you that the Earth or the people you love would be in real danger without your nightly battles in lucid dreams. This can go as far as waking up with scars, scratches, and pains in the body.

The energy that creates the personal resistance field will either want to scare you or give you what you want in the form of an illusion. It will not provide you with money, for example, but will make you believe that you will, one day, win the lottery. This energy will make you think that you will live the most fantastic life in the future. It will keep you dreaming about your prosperous future and waiting for it to happen instead of taking the actual steps necessary in the present time to build the future you wish for.

Realize that you are a reality writer, but you cannot write a thing if you are just floating in the enchanting clouds of the future, or swaddled in the dreamy arms of a hot, perfect lover that lives in your mind, or fighting never-ending astral plane galactic battles. Mastering and passing the personal resistance field was taught in mystery schools. Today, the curriculum has just been weaved perfectly into your life. Do an honest review of your life. Look at what is real and what is not, and summarize how much real (physical) time you invested in writing your reality and how much time you are physically investing to achieve your dreams?

How to do:

Test the energy (you can use the body pendulum technique)—Ask the energy three times if it comes from Love and Light. You must receive three positive affirmations that it does, so you know you are connecting with positive energy.

- Be present in your life.
- Be a doer.
- Go day by day.
- Stay positive.
- Self-love, self-care.
- Fall in love with yourself so the world can love you.
- Practice feeling unconditional love (you are loved unconditionally and can love unconditionally).

COLLECTIVE RESISTANCE

I am afraid of people, or I am frustrated with people and humanity. I prefer to be alone.

These beliefs are deeply hidden in your third chakra, and your ego echoes words like, "I do not trust people because they hurt me in the past. I am afraid of humanity. I am frustrated with their choices. I am

limited by my life circumstances. No one could understand my life and what I have been through."
Positive affirmation: *I accept humanity and respect their choices.*

Once you pass the personal resistance field, you will have more time to breathe and feel good. Depending on your journey, this may last a few weeks, months, or even years. During this period, you will work on changing your life and pursuing your dreams until you encounter collective resistance.

Did you ever want to shout at the top of your lungs to get your frustration out? Or lose it and yell at someone because you reached the last strand? That is precisely what the collective resistance does to you. It will make you sacrifice your energy and time for others who demand (or kindly ask) it of you (for their gain). There is nothing wrong with the act of kindness that you give by your free will; on the contrary, it is encouraged, but if someone pulls you in and suddenly you feel obligated to keep giving (because you are afraid to say no), then you are trapped in the resistance field.

Most likely, you will experience outbursts of frustration, anger, or despair with humanity that will literally punch you in the abdomen, or it could even feel like someone stabbed you with a knife. All this energy is just fear that you singlehandedly cannot control the outcome of where humanity is heading. You may also start feeling humanity's low-density collective emotions as your own. On top of it, whenever you find time for yourself for your particular project, everyone will have an emergency and demand your assistance. When that happens, just calm down and take a few deep breaths. It comes and leaves like a branch floating on the river.

You may start plunging every few months into three days of darkness called the dark night of the soul, but this time, you will be experiencing this on a collective humanity level. Going through spiritual rebirth will become routine instead of a rare mystical experience; some people may experience it daily. It could be exhausting and draining, and you could feel like you took on the negative karma of all humanity, and now it is up to you to cleanse it. This is not fun; you are just stuck in the circle of collective resistance. For how long will you cleanse the collective karma? How many rebirths do you need before you consciously decide you are done, and how long do you need to do this before you step out of the chaotic circle and take a few calming breaths?

At this level, this collective energy will physically offer you incentives to keep you busy so you are distracted from your mission to break through this field and be in service to humanity. For example, you may want to move to another city or state, have everything planned, and suddenly meet a new group of friends you always wished for. You tried to change your work and suddenly got an unexpected raise to keep you there. You wanted to meditate, and your husband rented a movie you expressed a few days ago you wanted to see to surprise you. This seems all positive, but if these things keep happening to keep you distracted from achieving your goal (literary holding you as a hostage), then they are just tricks from the collective energy field. Employ your intuition to distinguish which actions are signs to help you move forward and which are just incentives to keep you stagnant.

All these positive incentives are temporary, and you will return to the same old negative energy in no time. For example, the pay rise at work may not offer the new opportunities that the new job would offer. You would make more money at the old job, but you would not really grow.

View this false reality as an outsider looking in from a balcony. Collective resistance is actually hilarious. It can cause chaos, feelings like everyone is going crazy, people always needing something from you and not respecting your private time, misbehaving, or having problems, etc., or it can temporarily give you what you want. Just remember, you are passing through an energy barrier. Trust yourself and learn to trust the Universe. This field is just energy, not a monster that will tear you apart and swallow you if you say NO.

If you feel trapped in drama, chaos, or a life pattern, go onto that balcony and view the situation from a higher perspective. Set your intention that you are disconnecting your emotions from the problem; this way, whatever happens, will not emotionally hurt you. If you are not emotionally hurt, you are not drawn to participate. You will suddenly be able to see what is needed from you and what is not. You will see if there is something you can do or if you can respectfully stay back and not participate by choice. Naturally, those who were used to your selfless kindness and perhaps took advantage of you may try to guilt-trip, shame, bad-talk, and make you feel like you are such a bad person. If you were an angel while helping, how could you turn into this shameful black sheep when you decided to stop? You are still the same, correct? It does not make sense, does it? You must understand that you are not the same; you are someone who found the courage to stand up for yourself and others.

Stay focused on your task. There may be days when you feel discouraged, afraid, or like giving up. You may feel like you just want to crawl into your bed and sleep forever. The more afraid, angry, frustrated, etc., you are, the more difficult this barrier will be.

How to do:
- Focus on the present time.
- Focus on your tasks and daily activities.
- Set your boundaries and a specific time to work on your goals.
- Practice saying no when it is appropriate.
- Fall in love with humanity so humanity can fall in love with you.
- Practice daily rampage of gratitude and appreciation.
- Practice feeling peaceful.
- Practice observing your life from a higher perspective, and learn to see through the illusion.

- Connect with animals and nature.
- Learn to distinguish between what is helping you and what is holding you back.

COSMIC RESISTANCE

I am an orphan. I feel betrayed and abandoned by God.

These beliefs are deeply hidden in your fifth chakra and block your reprogramming ability. They are echoing with words like, "How do I know who is honest and speaks the truth? I do not have time for long-term changes. I feel generally discontent about life on Earth. I prefer to exit this incarnation cycle than to be in service to humanity."

Positive affirmation: *I surrender to the will of God, and I flow with cosmic energy.*

For affirmation, you can exchange the word God for your higher self, as your higher self is one with God.

When you pass the personal resistance phase, you choose unconditional love for yourself and others. Love is such a powerful energy. One who rises from fear to love cannot harm others, does not seek wars, and begins looking for a collective solution to improve this world. You can assist others by bringing knowledge and transformation when you pass the collective resistance field. You will fall back in love with humanity and enjoy being in service. This is crucial to your spiritual development, especially when striving toward your last incarnation. At this point, you will understand and embrace that you are a being of light living in a human body and that human life could be enjoyable. After all of this, you will enter the cosmic resistance phase.

The best way to describe cosmic resistance is to look into our past.

During Atlantis, we all enjoyed physical and spiritual highs and consciously altered natural life evolution. The original plan for extraterrestrial life on Earth was meant to be an isolated experiment without interfering with existing life. Thousands of years went by, and when early signs of possible destruction started appearing, many ignored them. Instead of being connected to the unity of the Cosmic Love and Universal Mind, many slowly disconnected from the higher guidance. Even the Children of the Law of One were only half connected to the higher guidance, as life on Earth offered such freedom and profound emotional and physical experiences, and we all were still searching for how God works. In other words, the extraterrestrials on Earth collectively (without putting blame on one side or other) created resistance in the cosmic energy.

Cosmic energy naturally flows in harmony, like a beautiful symphony. Also, remember that this Universe is perfectly disciplined and can be logically defined by the order of numbers.

This happened in Atlantis (and is sadly repeated many times in history): disharmony led to its destruction. We created a Surrogate God Crystal (to anchor our DNA) to have the ability to thrive on Earth. We did not do the proper research; we had not gained prior knowledge of how this could affect all of us, and thus, this project lacked any wisdom for the future. Instead, we created a shortcut so we could have our physical abundance. To do this, we contacted our genetic engineers, who could make what we were seeking. The goal was (for us) to have physical earthly bodies that would enable us to develop and do more physical things such as mining for gold and other riches, creating tools and machines, etc. The ability to physically create could be viewed as energy from the Universal Mind, while spiritual knowledge is considered the energy of Cosmic Love. In other words, Atlantis was overwhelmingly higher in technology and lower in spirituality. In this Universe, everything needs to be equally balanced. This is why Cosmic Love and the Universal Mind (as you read earlier) originally joined in oneness to test if this union could work together in harmony. We believed it could.

When someone or something creates a misbalance, the energy will naturally push toward correcting it so that harmony can be achieved again. The law of action and reaction applies to this whole Universe. It became apparent (to those tuned into spiritual laws) that Atlantis was heading for destruction. To be clear, no higher planetary beings planned the destruction. They invested so much in the Earth that they would never want it destroyed. They still feel the same. We all still have investments in the Earth's development, and that is why we love humanity and protect the Earth by all means.

Above all Universes, there is a higher force that keeps balance. For now, we will call that force Destiny. Navigating Destiny is like navigating a sailboat. You can set sail and be the master of your sea as long as you are in harmony with your environment and the cosmos and as long as you sail with the winds of Destiny and not against them.

As we already mentioned, you have the soul knowledge (memory) to change destiny, but it has to be aligned with the will of God's consciousness. God's energy is not a heartless ruler but loving parents (father and mother) who let you make your choices. If your choice is wrong, you fall and scrape your knees, but if your choice is correct, you soar like a bird.

In all universal life, there are moments when we all have to surrender to the will of God, no exceptions, because you are part of oneness, and oneness is God. When we alter destiny, which we could, it must not be for our, your, or my individual desire. Instead, it must be for the highest interest of all involved.

Therefore, as you learned from our story, cosmic resistance has a force that can destroy a whole continent or even a planet; however, you do not have to worry about that for now. You have passed from the collective resistance into the cosmic resistance field, and to flow freely with that cosmic energy, you must first restore your trust in a higher force. You must let go and allow your higher self to guide you on utilizing your unique skills to serve humanity. Remember, just as your higher self is one with God, you are one with God, and God is one with you.

When you experience resistance from this field, you will most likely notice that some eclectically powered objects, such as your computer, camera, phone, washer, etc., break down when you are upset or that the light bulbs around you blow up when your inner anger is about to explode. As amusing as it is, realizing that you can easily break electric/battery-powered things means you are just having a power struggle with the cosmic resistance field. You want things your way, and the cosmic energy intends to have its way. Once you notice this and surrender your wants and needs, the energy that breaks things will turn into the same level of positive energy that you can create. Your soul-mind consciousness is flowing with the cosmic field. It can destroy or create a whole population. This is why you sealed your energy in the Soul Cave, so neither you nor anyone else will abuse your god-like abilities.

How to do:
- Find your soul symbol. (we shared information on this in the previous book Pleiadian Code I, The Great Soul Rescue)
- Restore your trust in a higher force, in God.
- Meditate and ask how to be in service to humanity.
- Let go and let your higher self guide you.

- Practice going into the Soul Cave during meditation to access your soul memory. (as described later)

You may fluctuate between these levels until you master them. They are not considered to be a negative factor. Completing each level is like successfully completing mystery school initiations.

CHAPTER 11

OPENING THE SEAL

Meditation is a gateway to the unknown. It calms the ego and gives the soul wings to fly. ~ Pleiadians

We have created a meditation with step-by-step instructions to help you access your soul memory instead of providing a guide on opening the seal. It's important to remember that each person is unique and may require a different approach. Trust your intuition and have faith in yourself.

In chapter four, you practiced three energy exercises. The first was to connect with your body through the nervous system, the second was to accept unconditional love as your creative willpower, and the third was to learn the secret of manifesting. Build up on these skills, and allow for personal transformation while practicing the meditation given below. Work through your resistance fields until you feel you have reached the cosmic field and feel comfortable surrendering to the will of God (or your higher self, as you, too, are a god, whichever way you would like to phrase it). It may take time and practice to unseal your soul memory or happen on the first try. It truly depends on where you are in your spiritual journey. Just know that wherever you are, we have your back and are beside you.

Meditation:
1. Close your eyes and focus on your inward energy instead of connecting with everything around you. Take a deep breath and release all the air out. Repeat two more times until you feel calm and centered.
2. Say aloud or in your mind, *"I ask and thank you to be connected with the energy of God. I ask and thank you to be connected with my higher self. I ask and thank you to be connected with the frequency of unconditional love."*

Next, imagine being filled with unconditional love, starting from above your head and entering your head, neck, shoulders, arms, chest, back, belly, hips, and legs. Take your time and enjoy all this unconditional love within you.
3. Now, you will open your chakras. Say aloud or in your mind, *"I call upon the Atlantean crystal energy to connect with my whole being."*
- Breathe in the crystalline energy from the Earth and pull it into your first chakra. Imagine a rich red color expanding from inside out beyond your first chakra center.
- Breathe in the crystalline energy from the Earth and pull it into your second chakra. Imagine a bright orange color expanding from the inside out beyond your second chakra center.
- Breathe in the crystalline energy from the Earth and pull it into your third chakra. Imagine a shining yellow

color expanding from inside out beyond your third chakra center.

- Breathe in the crystalline energy from the Earth and pull it into your fourth chakra. Imagine a fresh green color expanding from inside out beyond your fourth chakra center.

- Breathe in the crystalline energy from the Earth and pull it into your fifth chakra. Imagine a soothing sky-blue color expanding from the inside out beyond your fifth chakra center.

- Breathe in the crystalline energy from the Earth and pull it into your sixth chakra. Imagine a deep midnight blue color expanding from inside out beyond your sixth chakra center.

- Breathe in the crystalline energy from the Earth and pull it into your seventh chakra. Imagine a cosmic violet color expanding from inside out beyond your seventh chakra center. Now imagine this energy extending out and connecting with Alcyone in the Pleiades.

4. Now return to your heart, your fourth chakra, which is the seat of your soul. Put both palms of your hands over your heart and accept the fact that you are a star being currently living in a human body. Say out aloud or in your mind: *"I accept myself. I accept this human vessel as a bodily vehicle for this incarnation. I am worthy. I unconditionally love my whole self (physical and spiritual)."*

Now, send out energy waves of unconditional love, starting in your heart and expanding into your whole body. Take three slow, deep breaths and feel your body saturated in unconditional love. With each breath you take, breathe in the following affirmation and breathe it out into your auric field:

"I am unconditional love."

"I am unconditional love."

"I am unconditional love."

5. Next, move the palms of your hands to your stomach, your third chakra. Meet your fearless partner, your ego. Say aloud or in your mind, *"Dear Ego, thank you for protecting me. I love you. From now on, can we work as equal partners and take a leap of faith together? Could we, as a team, forgive humanity?"*

(If you feel your ego agrees, continue with the next steps. If not, stop here and focus your spiritual work on healing your human ego, and return to this journey when you feel ready.)

"I accept humanity and respect their free will choices, despite their consequences. I am here to assist those who want to be helped. I love humanity."

Now, send out waves of peaceful energy, starting in your stomach and expanding into your whole body. Take three slow, deep breaths and feel your body saturated in peaceful, serene energy. With each breath you take, breathe in the following affirmation and breathe it out into your auric field:

"I accept humanity and respect their free will choices."

"I accept humanity and respect their free will choices."

"I accept humanity and respect their free will choices."

6. Next, move the palms of your hands to your neck, your fifth chakra. From now on, your ego walks with you on your path. You have entered the dark room, and you both have to trust the higher guidance of God. Say aloud or in your mind: *"I surrender to the will of God."* Feel the unconditional love of God vibrating in every cell of your being. Allow yourself to be guided to hidden windows within this dark room. Locate the blackout shutters with intuition, open them, and let the light shine in. From now on, your ego and you are loved, and light will always guide you on your path.

Now send out energy waves of absolute trust, starting in your neck and expanding into your whole body. Take three slow, deep breaths and feel your body saturated in absolute trust. With each breath you take, breathe in the following affirmation and breathe it out into your auric field:

"I trust my higher self, and I surrender to the will of God."

"I trust my higher self, and I surrender to the will of God."

"I trust my higher self, and I surrender to the will of God."

7. Next, move the palms of your hands over your first chakra. This is where your ego and you face all your possible fears. Remember, you hold the frequency of love, and light shines down your path.

Affirm aloud or in your mind: *"I am safe."*

There is nothing to be afraid of because you trust the guidance of God. Love is the miraculous frequency that will lead you into the opening of your Soul Cave.

Now send out energy waves of feeling safe, starting in your first chakra and expanding into your whole body. Take three slow, deep breaths and feel your body saturated in the energy of feeling safe. With each breath you take, breathe in the following affirmation and breathe it out into your auric field:

"I am safe."

"I am safe."

"I am safe."

8. Now, imagine that you are walking out of your body. Imagine walking on a slightly curved path, starting at the bottom of your feet and continuing upward until you reach a point just above your head. Do not let anything intimidate you on this journey. Whatever you may see is just an illusion to keep you distracted. Once you reach the point above your head, you have found your Soul Cave.

Using your soul symbol, open the door to your cave. You are the only one, for now and always, who is permitted to walk inside. Your Soul Cave is abundant in crystals, and each crystal represents one of your past lives on Earth. Focus your intention on finding where you have hidden your soul memory. Your soul memory will be hidden in an ancient artifact; you can only access it when you feel worthy.

Say out aloud or in your mind: *"I am worthy to embody my soul memory."*

Locate the hidden ancient artifact. When you are ready, open it. If it opens effortlessly, then you are worthy of retrieving your soul memory. If it does not open, just meditate with your object. Holding it will give you enough energy to work on your soul's growth. When your object opens, you will see or sense a turquoise-colored essence of yourself. This is the extraterrestrial consciousness that you used during your life on Earth. This is your soul memory. Breathe slowly and deeply the essence of the turquoise color. Take as much time as you need during this step.

9. When ready, you will bring this essence into your body. Walk out of the cave. The cave closes behind you. Remember, you are still out of your body.

- Consciously step into your mind, automatically activating the pineal gland. Say aloud or in your mind, *"I surrender to the will of God."*

- Next, step down into your throat. Say aloud or in your mind, *"I accept humanity and their choices."*

- Lastly, step down into your heart and say aloud or in your mind, "I am love. I am the Temple of Truth."

10. Focus on your heart chakra and allow your turquoise essence to download its consciousness into your human heart. Breathe in slowly and deeply. Feel the connection from your heart (your central sun) with the solar disk above your head (representing your Soul Cave) and the central sun.

11. Record all of this in your nervous system. Put your left hand on your bladder (second chakra) and your right hand on your mind's eye (sixth chakra). Take several slow, full breaths in and out, and focus just on your breathing. You are in the energy of now. Imagine the turquoise essence merging with your whole being through your nervous system. You may feel a slight electric buzzing through your body. Pay attention to how it feels to be present in your body.

12. Welcome back, divine being of light; we have been waiting for you.

13. Express your gratitude to everyone who assisted you on this journey. Thank you. Thank you. Thank you.

CHAPTER 12

THE WHEEL THAT KEEPS SPINNING

Eyes are the doorway to the soul-mind consciousness.
~ Pleiadians

Ancient symbolism is encoded everywhere on Earth to remind you of your soul memories. They are not hidden in difficult-to-find places but in plain sight. You can find ancient paintings and engravings on the walls of caves, pyramids, and many sacred sites. You can also see them on ancient stones, pottery, or jewelry. They have survived the test of time and are everywhere for you to see.

Throughout this book, we have consciously used four keywords: **knowledge, wisdom, soul memory,** and **abundance**. Each word represents a particular energy. These four specific words can be found in one symbol. The symbol consists of a circle containing a cross, which divides the circle into four identical parts. Each end of the cross extends beyond the circle and is shaped like a spiral. Two spirals generate an infinite symbol. Since the cross has four sides, there are four spirals. They are interconnected only in the center, like a lucky four-leaf clover, empowering one another.

These four equal parts have similar energy to the four seasons of the year, the four cardinal directions, the four elements, or the four tarot suits. Symbols are a universal language.

Earth's different languages vary in the sound of these four keywords, yet the meaning remains the same throughout the entire Universe. Each word gives meaning to a particular energy that is a foundation for the next. One connects to the other, one step at a time, in a clockwise motion, starting with knowledge at the southern point (**knowledge → wisdom → soul memory → abundance**) until the whole circle is established. When this circle is activated, it is like an electric circuit that lights the light bulbs. This energy vortex can be created by an individual or collective effort. Since it is energy (which does not discriminate who uses it), it could be positive or negative, depending on the intention. Knowing the true meaning of these words and working with their combined energy could lead you toward accessing your pre-flood consciousness (your soul memory). This is an old Atlantean teaching that the Children of the Law of One worked with, as did Sons Belial because they all desired a spiritual or physical abundance or both.

KNOWLEDGE

The circle begins to generate its energy at its southern point. Knowledge is the cornerstone. One day, you will be inspired by an idea, such as changing your profession. Your willingness to do this ignites the fire within you to transform your life. You are ready to put all your best effort into accomplishing your goal, but first, you must gather enough information to learn how to do it. You have free will to choose how to obtain the knowledge you need.

Naturally, research is essential to gathering the necessary knowledge so you can learn and plan. Learning and planning reduce the stress and anxiety associated with the upcoming changes you will face. You are in a stage of transformation that needs a lot of grounding energy. Working with your ego (your human self) is essential to ensure that the ego will assist you in this task. Every change unsettles the ego as it is always afraid of how it will continue to protect you during these changes. Teach your human ego to feel safe, and that change is good.

Connect with nature, practice to still your mind, and do not rush to reach your destination. Patience is also a part of this foundation. The knowledge you gain intellectually must also connect with your intuitive emotions. When you connect the knowing and feeling, you are closer to manifesting anything you desire.

Imagine that your idea is a bit tiny seed of a tree. Hold your seed in your hands and express your love for it. Then, metaphorically, plant it on the Earth, anywhere you like. While doing this, connect with Mother Earth

153

(Mineral Kingdom, Plant Kingdom, and Animal Kingdom) and ask them for help growing your seed. Express your gratitude for their generous assistance. Next, while connected with the Earth, ask for the knowledge of the ancients on how to nourish your seed (your idea) so it can grow into a strong tree. Spend time with your growing tree and use your intuition to learn all you can.

Earth contains records of ancient knowledge. It is also buzzing with inner cities occupied by various intelligent extraterrestrial beings. You never know who will come to your aid. Pay attention to all the signs. There is no such thing as a coincidence. While asking for help, you must be persistent and patient until you convince them (by your selfless actions) that your intentions are sincere and that the knowledge you receive will assist humanity. Any work you choose could be centered on assisting humanity (teacher, doctor, car maker, gardener, seamstress, cook, etc.).

Most of all, stay present in your life. Do not get lost in thinking why this will not work because of something that went wrong in the past. If something from the past emerges, heal it; do not dwell on it. And do not get trapped in a dreamy future. Stay in now and gather as much knowledge as possible to allow your seed to grow.

WISDOM

Out of knowledge, wisdom is born. You know that knowledge is a great power, but power without wisdom is only temporary. Sit in the crown of your tree. Spend some time hanging out with Mother Earth, especially watching the sunset. Appreciate the magical play of colors in the sky as the sun comes down after a whole day of traveling from east to west. Even at the end of its day's journey, it still shares its best with you. Review your day, what went well and what did not. Be honest with yourself, and let go of all disappointment, frustration, and anger if you are harboring it. Learn to communicate clearly about ideas and goals. This will nourish the seed you planted and assist with its growth. Miscommunication causes so many misunderstandings and hurt feelings. Express gratitude for your day and for everything that has happened.

When the sun rests beyond the horizon, welcome the darkness of the night and allow your soul to walk in it. Your past or past lives may have been traumatizing, but it was not darkness that harmed you. It was people manipulated or victimized by other people or malevolent beings. Darkness heals because it allows for your mind to be still. Only fear keeps it anxious, suggesting that the dark night is your enemy. On the contrary, you can hide better in the darkness from anyone who may want to harm you than in daylight.

The only way to put your knowledge to use is by trying it in your everyday life and determining what works for you and what does not. This is how you find wisdom. Wisdom is refined knowledge. It is a unique part of who you are and will define your life mission. You may have a lot of knowledge on several subjects, but only by utilizing it will you discover what you are truly good at and passionate about. For example, you may have a lot of knowledge about healing. You practice it but then feel unfulfilled while giving one-on-one healing. Instead of dooming your healer's career, you may teach a group of people how to do the healing. You may enjoy being a teacher more than a healer. You discover all this about yourself while putting your knowledge to work in real life. Your wisdom may vary from other people, and if you learn to respect that, you avoid conflicts. If you have a bad day, always remember that the sun will rise again in the morning, and you will have a whole new day to be the reality writer of your life. It is up to you to decide what kind of day you will have.

SOUL MEMORY

The white snow covers the land to the north, and freezing temperatures discourage everyone from visiting. To the north is the Soul Cave that hides your soul memory (your full extraterrestrial consciousness). You have hidden it by yourself, and YOU will be the only one capable of reclaiming it when you are ready. In the meantime, practice to be present in your life. Allow your emotions to heal, believe in yourself, restore your trust in the Universe and yourself, and find your worthiness.

Your soul memory is like a double-edged sword. Since Earth is a place of amplified duality, you need to grow into your soul memory instead of having it given to you as a birthright. In the beginning, you may receive only little bits and pieces to assist you in manifesting your ideas. It is a test of how well you will do with it. The amount is not necessary. Even the tiniest droplet of your soul memory is a downpour in your Earth life. Keep working with this energy, and you will cultivate more of it. Still, please remember that your soul memory is a powerful weapon and equally creative as it is destructive, and so is your abundance, knowledge, and wisdom.

Many of you have this unexplained feeling that if you truly stand in your power, you may harm others, not intentionally but accidentally. This is a significant blockage. When you fear your soul memory, you block your abundance.

You already know that only you are in charge of your soul energy. No one can attach implants, blockages, or controlling energy to it without your free will agreement. You created restrictions on using your soul memory before fully understanding its function in the human body. You have programmed this energy so that you will fear your power until you are spiritually evolved enough to utilize unconditional love as your creative willpower. You hoped to prevent your accidental misuse of this energy to manipulate others or get what YOU want while not fully conscious. We are giving you the first step, the knowledge, and it is up to you to apply it toward your soul's mastery.

ABUNDANCE

The future is now. Spring is in full bloom, and Earth awakens to the sounds of new life. You may think that abundance will come during the harvest in the fall, but it arrives in the spring. Before you celebrate your achievements, pay it forward. Plant new seeds for humanity and yourself so spring may always sprout new life. Keep the circles of life going.

Metaphorically said, each seed will activate its coded knowledge on how to grow, and the tiny sprout will thrive because it acquired wisdom from previous experiences. It will not be afraid of days without water because it knows that the older trees, with their big roots below the Earth's surface, will reach out to the baby tree and share their nourishment with it. Mother Earth will do her best to protect her child, and Father Universe will do the same. A little tree will abandon its fear and grow into a giant tree with the power to share with others. Abundance will be poured to everyone who will find peace around this tree. It will offer shelter and perhaps even food. It will also connect and communicate with the inner Earth and the Universe. The tree will share many seeds, and the air will carry them to faraway places where they may settle and someday grow to become giant trees. Animals will come by and take these seeds to even further places. The abundance will grow year after year. One tree can make a forest.

Abundance itself is neutral energy. Depending on your choices, you may manifest positive or negative abundance. On Earth, you have unlimited access to spiritual and material abundance. After all, you are a reality writer who could thrive in the physical realm. Therefore, you have been blessed with the birthright of being a creator to teach others a good, honest way of life. Build shelters, grow food, make clothes, build cars, etc. There are no limits on what you can do. But anything you do, do from your heart. When you live from your heart, following this simple guide, you create a positively abundant conscious community around you. You are changing the world.

Positive abundance is manifested from knowledge.

Negative abundance is manifested from the hunger for power, lack of knowledge, and shortcuts.

Knowledge is everywhere to find. It is easy to gain, and it is your cornerstone. The hardest part is persevering to put your expertise to work. Excuses will not yield wisdom. Wisdom is gained by sometimes exhausting trial and error, letting go, and letting God guide you. The guidance will lead you into your Soul Cave, where the warm sun rays of your soul memory surface, causing the frozen, snow-covered river to defrost. The tiny stream will become a mighty river filled with life-enhancing water, and everyone who drinks from your Well of Wisdom will be blessed with good health, happiness, abundance, and unconditional love.

CHAPTER 13

SIGNIFICANCE OF EARTH'S ENERGY

Minerals have the highest intelligence of any life on Earth. Ancient aliens knew this and used it to their advantage. ~ Pleiadians

The Mineral Kingdom, Plant Kingdom, and Animal Kingdom were established on Earth before any alien life set foot on it. They evolved through natural evolution until the first extraterrestrial experiment started. Once you learn how to access your soul memory, your energy will transform into 5D while still living in 3D, and you will be able to connect deeply with these three realms and other planetary beings, especially through Mineral Kingdom.

MINERAL KINGDOM

Earth is embedded with mineral deposits in various depths below the surface. Some are so deep that your science has yet to discover them. These deposits also vary significantly in size. Since this Universe was created in mathematical code, you can imagine that these mineral deposits are strategically positioned inside the Earth to create an inner energy grid you call the crystalline grid. This grid supports the Earth's life for the duration of its existence. It also makes a magnetic shield around the Earth to protect it from solar radiation. From space or your psychic vision, it appears as if Earth is wrapped in a loose crocheted blanket made with perfectly defined geometric lines. The mineral energy from inside the Earth projects this hologram outside the Earth for everyone to see.

Minerals have intelligent mind consciousness. They grow and are immortals! Though some can dissolve in water, they do not die or decompose. When that happens, they do not disappear; their energy value simply transmutes into water.

Minerals can be programmed. This means that the whole Earth's crystalline grid could be programmed. Crystals are already commonly used in electronics and technology and can be used for (or by) AI. The natural energy they have could be used for positive or negative purposes, depending on the mind that programs them.

The crystalline grid produces magnificent energy that forms ley lines, vortexes and stargates, depending on the minerals in that area.

The ancient cultures knew all of this and tailored their ceremonies based on what kind of mineral deposit was below the Earth to support their intention. For example, you would not initiate a heart opening ceremony on a black tourmaline deposit location. The black tourmaline energy is grounding and protective (suited for shamanic work) but not supportive for diving into your heart's emotions. A watermelon tourmaline deposit or rose quartz would be much more suitable for that.

The ancients (after-flood civilization) did not drill holes in the Earth to test what minerals they would find at particular sites. Instead, they would intuitively connect with Mother Earth, communicate with her, and sense what kind of energy was emanating from that location. Energy has its own language.

Ancient aliens (pre-flood civilizations) had technology that allowed them to look inside the Earth with what could be compared to X-ray technology. With this technology, they would know where these high-energy areas were located before they began building their sacred sites. Some vortexes and stargates were used to reenergize their batteries for space travel, some for interstellar communication, and others for spiritual and healing practices. When the aliens were mining for gold, they used the same technology to locate suitable deposits. They did not just mine with the hope that they would find gold; they knew precisely where it was located and how deep it was.

LEY LINES

All mineral deposits of a significant size work as natural amplifiers, connecting to one another despite long distances. Just as the roots of trees are connected to one another (and could energetically support one another even at long distances), so are these minerals in a very organized fashion. Connections between mineral deposits create what you call Ley lines. Ley lines are consciously connected, invisible energy that carries energy back and forth between mineral deposits. No aliens or humans can artificially reproduce this. Ancient aliens and ancient cultures built around these lines because they knew how to use this amplifying energy for their benefit. Energy is invisible, pliable, and transformative. When you have knowledge of this energy, you can use it for anything.

VORTEX AND STARGATE

Crossing lay lines creates an energy vortex. Two or more connected vortexes can generate stargate energy. A stargate can also be found on the mineral deposit consisting of various minerals (think, for example, of rainbow tourmaline). It produces a combination of energy that can easily support all your seven chakra centers. A stargate generates significant 7D energy, especially when aligned with the sun's energy on auspicious days such as the Solstices, or Pleiadian alignments, etc. This energy was used for regenerative healing, accessing hidden knowledge, and interplanetary communication. You can think of this energy as an unlimited Wi-Fi connection that allows communication with the whole Universe. Other planets have their stargates, and since we all are connected through the central sun, the sun is like a modem for this Wi-Fi interplanetary connection.

During the time of Lemuria and Atlantis, we did not need stargates or vortexes, as we had all the sophisticated technology required for communication, interplanetary travel, and regenerative healing. However, after the destruction of Atlantis, when we became temporary stuck on Earth, we had to improvise and learn to use Earth's natural resources. We focused on stargates and vortexes to restore interplanetary communication.

Stargates are the keepers of knowledge, or you can call it a library of knowledge. They energetically collect and store records (like a hard drive). Since they are connected directly to the Mineral Kingdom, they are beneficial in providing access to the whole history of the Earth. When a stargate is connected via the central sun, you can access the Universal Mind, which holds galactic knowledge. Once again, it is like going to the library.

Any knowledge obtained from a stargate enters your body through your nervous system as a spiritual download. Pre-flood, genetically modified extraterrestrial bodies could handle such energy and decipher messages in the Language of Light. After the flood, human bodies need to be prepared for this. Thus, the ancients underwent many initiations and training to hold this cosmic energy in their bodies and comprehend its meaning without compromising their nervous systems and mental health.

HEALING TEMPLES

Healing temples were built near stargates, preferably in caves. A skilled healer at the Rejuvenating Temple would direct mineral (Earthly energy) and cosmic energy into the body for physical rejuvenation (the body requires both energies).

At present, you enjoy using crystals in your healing routines. You can learn to communicate with them and ask them to be connected (for the reason needed) to their family within Earth. Upon asking, your minerals will establish the long-distance connection, giving a tiny, tumbled stone the power of a giant. You can then create a healing temple at your house or feel guidance on where to create one. Experiment and play with them. Become a friend to them. Minerals have the highest intelligence of any life on Earth, including extraterrestrials living in the human body because they have direct connection to the Universal Mind.

HEALING WATER

On Earth, you also have bodies of water at specific locations with significant healing properties. This water sits on healing mineral deposits, and the healing comes from the mineral energy directly connecting with the water and, in some cases, dissolving into the water. Since water is a natural amplifier, it turns this energy into a miraculous healing solution. Animals intuitively know this, and if they live near one of these areas, you will see them soaking their wounds in the water. If you observe these healings, you will find that the healing process is speedy and can occur within a few days rather than several weeks. Ancient tribes observed this, mimicked these animals, and found the secret of the healing waters.

STRENGTHENING YOUR CONNECTION

Look into your mineral collection and pick the crystal that speaks to you the most, which you feel you want to hold by your heart. Spend some time with this crystal, take it with you into nature, and make a deep soul connection. You do not have to be afraid that you will be stuck in the incarnation cycle when connecting with the Earth and its minerals. On the contrary, it will assist to propel you to places you desire to go. Connecting with the inner Earth is not a step backward. It is a massive leap of faith forward, especially when it is your last incarnation.

The crystal you picked may become your tool for healing and assist with all the topics we covered in this book about how to heal the ancient alien within you. Meditate with your crystal often and ask that it connect with a mineral deposit within the Earth (with its soul family). In your imagination, let the crystal carry you to this location into the inner Earth. Do not try to control it; just let your astral body and mind flow freely. Once you are energetically ready (when your ego is your friend instead of your protector, the Mineral Kingdom will guide you toward a mineral energy vortex or a stargate. At this point, *you may be asked to become a guardian of this vortex or stargate (the guardian of Earth)* and you will be directly connected to its vast mineral deposit. It is a great honor to be bestowed with this task. If you accept, you will be responsible for keeping your energy clear, positive, and connected to the field of Cosmic Love and to the chosen mineral deposit. Remember, you will not choose to be the guardian. It will choose you, and it is up to you to accept or decline its invitation. This is a great honor.

As a guardian, you will become a conscious connector between Earth's so-called lowest realm and this Universe's highest realm. Through you, the light of the crystalline grid of Earth will consciously connect with the love of Cosmic Love. YOU are the heavenly bodily vehicle to make this connection happen – with your genuine intention and selfless desire to be in service.

The guardian energy will work as a torus of energy rising from the Earth, going through your body, expanding into the Universe, and then returning to Earth. At this point, *you will be responsible for energizing the Earth's crystalline grid with unconditional love*. Unconditional love lacks any control, helps the truth to thrive, and love makes the mind happy. **Happy mind creates happy reality.** Supply the Earth with loving, positive energies and cleanse her from all negative energies that she may be affected by from previous conflicts, greed for power, wars, etc. Repeat this often, making it an effortless daily routine. You may feel that you are the only one doing this, but that is untrue. Ask for your vortex or stargate (that you are the guardian of) to consciously connect with others. Your soul-mind consciousness can direct this energy when you ask. As you already know, each vortex and stargate is connected to Earth's Ley lines. Imagine that your vortex or stargate is like a Wi-Fi hotspot to connect to with other star-seeds stationed on Earth who accepted the same job as you – to be the **guardian of Earth**. This is teamwork, not a solo mission. The power of collective work and intention is incredible, and it is bestowed upon you. **The crystalline grid is programmable, and love is the most powerful energy to program it with.**

MIND CONTROL

Every type of energy on Earth has two sides, positive and negative. The Earth's crystalline grid is no different. Its energy flow could amplify positive endeavors as well as harmful endeavors. It is just energy, and energy does not discriminate who uses it.

The Sons of Belial started to experiment with this in Sumeria after creating slave human beings. When humans were given the right to reproduce, the Sons of Belial programmed specific mineral energy centers with negative energy to keep them entrapped in fear so they would never grow into their extraterrestrial consciousness, which was the seed of light their creation. This all worked like for example a dog's electric collar works today. Of course, the technology back then was much more sophisticated, so there was no need for a physical collar. Instead, they energetically connected humans' second chakra to a chosen part of the Ley line to keep them under emotional control. Their sixth chakra has been connected to this grid as well, and through poisoning of the mind with fearful messages, the humans freely gave up their power and surrendered to a life of suffering.

In the book Pleiadian Code I, The Great Soul Rescue, we share that your second, fourth, and sixth chakras are your cosmic/spiritual energy chakras. They operate from your soul energy. Your first, third, fifth, and seventh chakras are your physical energy chakras operating from your ego's energy. The Sons of Belial intentionally targeted control of the cosmic/spiritual chakras so that human beings could not connect with their original soul energy.

Notice that many places of worship are built on the powerful Ley lines. Messages delivered from these places to those who trust a particular authority could be easily used to enlighten or manipulate and instill fear. Fear, anger, unhappiness, greed, violent energy, etc., are all harvested from human beings through the second chakra and directed to program the crystalline grid (the part chosen to control humans) with this negative energy. It became self-charging. At the same time, the mind program is fed through the sixth chakra.

Pay attention to this: knowing (6th chakra) + feeling (2nd chakra) connection, a recipe for manifestation in 3D. When learning to disconnect and manifest, you should use a 3D manifesting formula before upgrading to 5D to train your nervous system to sustain this energy. When you use this consciously, you become in control instead of someone controlling you.

When you are not consciousness, the Sons of Belial are using the same formula and guiding you in creating your own suffering. They are feeding you with fearful knowledge and then may give you suggestions on how to protect yourself by possibly doing harm to yourself or others. This naturally amplifies your low vibrational emotions. Feeling shame, guilt, or apathy is like golden music for their grid. They have you hooked to their negative grid because this energy is used for the mind control of humanity. Fear motivates survival. Suffering influences creative willpower. You create to survive.

One, two, or three beings cannot produce enough energy to energize the crystalline grid with positive or negative energy to control others. If you can influence a whole nation and convince them, for example, to fear change, the fear will produce obedient sheep, and the self-energizing job will be done. Once in a while, a few sheep may want to break free, but you have (metaphorically) a remote control (and an electric dog collar) that will direct negative energy from the crystalline grid to the sheep, amplifying their weakness (everyone has some) and keeping them fenced in the chosen reality. Remember, every fence has a gate.

This is how it works. When you want to break free from this control, the positive energy enters your body via the second chakra as a desire for freedom. When you start enjoying this feeling of possible freedom, an alarm warns of the possible escape. At this point, negative energy, set in place to keep you captive, will begin to spread throughout your nervous system like a virus (suggested fearful or angry negative thoughts). From there, it will travel to your spine until it reaches your mind. On its journey, it will compromise /paralyze your Vagus nerve and suggest negative or self-destructive thoughts directed toward yourself or possibly others. Since you have hidden fears and weaknesses and often feel bad over something that happened in the past (it is normal), it is relatively easy to control you like this. This is just a basic, simple explanation. The bottom line is that you may be influenced by an energy that amplifies and controls your fears. *However, you can control this*

172

energy with your free will choice with deciding on how you will feel. This takes practice! Natural crystalline grid energy is neutral and only amplifies what you have within. It can amplify both love and fear in equal measure.

DISCONNECTION

To disconnect from this controlling grid, you must first understand how it works and to yourself. Become familiar with your weaknesses and fears, which are hidden within you. Be bold to identify them. Knowledge is power. Write them down so you can consciously understand them. When you bring light into darkness, there is nothing to fear. The next step in your disconnection is to practice being present in your life. Focus on what you really want and start un-inviting what you (or your ancestors) may have benevolently invited within.

"I am un-inviting energy, entities, spirits, beings, and frequencies attached to me/connected to me that are not with the will of God's consciousness. Go to God. Go to the light. Or return to Earth. I chose to disconnect from the negative crystalline grid and reconnected to the positive crystalline grid." (You can choose to connect to the Christ/Magdalene crystalline grid.)

The whole process may take some time. Keep repeating it and be persistent. Nourish your nervous system and pay attention when negative energy tries to gain your attention and sneak back in through the gate of the second chakra. If that happens, just repeat the process. Remember, fall in love with the human you are, accept the alien within, and enjoy serving humanity until you are ready to go home. With this kind of mind, nothing can control you.

IN CONCLUSION, the future is in your hands. The New Earth you dream about is not a separate vehicle you will board at the next station. The Old Earth is the New Earth. Your body is part of the New Earth. The Earth is here to stay. It is not going anywhere.

Earth is constantly changing, evolving, and no one can stop that. At this time, you are heading into a technologically advanced age. It is crucial to awaken your heart and assist your inventors, engineers, doctors, scientists, teachers, lawmakers, and everyone else you meet to do the same.

Work from the heart instead of the mind so that the well-being of Earth and humanity is always the number one priority and in harmony with soul-mind consciousness. The human being is marvelous, intelligent, kind, loving, caring, and compassionate. It can hold many emotions from the lowest to the highest. It is a gift that needs to be understood. When technology becomes more intelligent than you, treat AI as your helpful friend instead of outsourcing your power to it.

You have something rare that AI will never have – the soul's emotions and unconditional love, which is not programmable. If you are naturally in control of your feelings (your soul), you control your life and your journey back home.

The time of the past and the future is now. You are the reality writer, and we are the bringers of the knowledge.

We love you unconditionally ~ Pleiadians

ABOUT THE AUTHOR

Eva Marquez is a spiritual consultant, soul healer, guide, teacher, TM Sidha, and writer with a Pleiadian star-seed lineage. She has authored six books and appeared on Gaia TV's "Beyond Belief." She works alongside her guides, the Lights of the Universe, a group of light beings from different star nations, including the Pleiades. In her spiritual practice, she draws on Pleiadian energy, the Language of Light, and other ancient soul memories.

Eva and her team help star-seeds remember their past lives on Earth and beyond, activate their dormant cosmic DNA, and reconnect with their soul family. She strives to aid star-seeds in adapting to their physical bodies, empowering them to fulfill their life missions in supporting humanity's evolution into a multidimensional species while safeguarding the planet for future generations.

Eva brings the memories of infinite love – the essence of God's Source – the most profound energy that is your original essence. She walks beside you on your life journey, assisting you in letting go of your fears of darkness and limitations and seeing the light at the end of the tunnel. Ultimately, she guides you to the point where infinite love is no longer a memory but your guide. Infinite love will become your friend on the journey toward the light of your origin. Love and light give birth to the wisdom that is a compass for the soul-mind consciousness on the healing journey of returning home to its original source. It is Eva's greatest wish that you find your way home.

Learn more about Eva and her services and classes:
   www.EvaMarquez.org

Visit Eva's YouTube channel: Eva Marquez

OTHER BOOKS BY EVA MARQUEZ

Activate Your Cosmic DNA: Discover Your Starseed Family from the Pleiades, Sirius, Andromeda, Centaurus, Epsilon Eridani, and Lyra

Soul Cleansing and Energetic Protection : Removing Negative Energies and Entities, Earthbound and Extraterrestrial

Pleiadian Code I: The Great Soul Rescue

Pleiadian Code II: Cosmic Love

Pleiadian Code III : Alien Fragment

Embody Your Cosmic DNA: Become Multidimensional, Find Your Soulmate

ONE LAST THING

If you liked this book, I would be grateful if you could leave a brief review on Amazon. Your support means a lot to me, and I read every review. Thank you for being so supportive!

Love and Light,
Eva Marquez

Made in the USA
Las Vegas, NV
04 September 2024

94804858R00105